Special Features – How to Use This Companion Book

Welcome to Training The Street's (TTS) Companion Book to Fundamentals of Financial Accounting & Analysis Handbook authored by Stephen H. Bryan, Ph.D. In the Handbook we discussed many of the common accounting, reporting and financial analysis issues encountered by professionals required to understand and analyze financial information—from investment bankers and financial analysts to corporate managers and executives.

Some of the best ways to illustrate and help reinforce the Handbook's analysis techniques are to walk through an analysis of a real firm and with practice exercises. Therefore, this Companion Book has two parts:

1) **Real World Analysis Case Study** – A real world analysis exercise involving actual an actual public firm's financial statements as well as the resulting analysis techniques used by many professionals. Included in this section are also step-by-step instructions to locating information on the internet plus a comparison of the case study firm to its nearest competitor.

2) **Practice Exercises (and Solutions)** – Over 150 practice exercises and knowledge checks to complement the Handbook lessons and solidify your learning experience. This section is organized chapter by chapter to follow the content delivered in the Handbook. Once you've challenged yourself, check and see if you got the correct answers!

Please check our website at **www.trainingthestreet.com** for other self-study products and live instruction alternatives such as Corporate Valuation, Financial Modeling, Excel Best Practices and many more to come.

About the Author – Stephen H. Bryan, Ph. D.

Professor Bryan has a Ph.D. in Accounting from New York University's Stern School of Business, as well as M.B.A. and B.S. degrees from Baruch College (City University of New York) and from the University of North Carolina-Chapel Hill, respectively. He is currently on the faculty at Fordham University Schools of Business in New York. Prior tenured faculty positions include Wake Forest University (Winston Salem, North Carolina), and Baruch College. While at Wake Forest, Dr. Bryan led numerous summer business study trips to Central and Eastern Europe. He has designed accounting and finance curricula for financial institutions, law firms, and multinational corporations. He has also had visiting positions on faculties in Vienna, Austria and Frankfurt, Germany.

Professor Bryan's research interests focus on corporate disclosures and corporate governance, and his research has been published in some of the leading academic and professional journals, including the Journal of Corporate Finance, the Accounting Review, the Journal of Business, Harvard Business Review, Financial Management, The Accountants' Handbook, and the Journal of Accounting, Auditing, and Finance. His teaching has been recognized with several awards, including the Kienzle award (from Wake Forest University), which alumni award to the faculty member who most benefited their careers. He is founder and principal of Accounting Analytics, LLC and The Accounting Oasis, LLC, which design and produce curricular materials on accounting issues currently confronting the analyst community and other user groups. Professor Bryan also delivers live seminars as an instructor for TTS. He can be reached at *Stephen.Bryan@TheAccountingOasis.com*.

This Companion Book, "Real World Analysis & Exercises", and the Handbook "Fundamentals of Financial Accounting & Analysis", are compilations of topics selected by TTS and Professor Bryan to get readers up to speed quickly. For the expanded and complete versions of the Companion and the Handbook, please visit Professor Bryan's website *www.theaccountingoasis.com*.

Part 1: Real World Exercise – Analysis of Lowe's Companies, Inc.

BEFORE WE BEGIN

When describing a firm, analysts often use the term "story." For instance, the firm we will study, Lowe's Companies, Inc., is an interesting "story." Lowe's is a U.S. "specialty retailer" that sells products and services for the home. It has over 40,000 products, sourced all over the globe, many of which are high-end tools and appliances. It has historically targeted the DIY ("do-it-yourself") shopper, but it has increasingly pursued the DIFM ("do-it-for-me") market. This latter market consists of customers who will shop at Lowe's for the product, but who also buy Lowe's installation service. For instance, we might go to Lowe's and buy products for the bathroom, but not too many of us may be keen to install a shower or sink. Instead, we would contract with Lowe's for them to do it for us.

When we describe a firm's size, we typically refer to revenues. Thus we would describe Lowe's as a $48.2 billion firm, which is the amount of Lowe's revenues for the most recent year. Lowe's has had tremendous success, growing rather quickly over the years with relatively little need for outside financing. Its growth, as we will see, has largely been funded with internally generated capital (cash flow).

In this section, we take a tour through Lowe's 10-K, which is the primary annual filing at the Securities and Exchange Commission (SEC). Lowe's Financial Statements are relatively "plain vanilla" which is one contributing factor for our choosing this firm as an introductory case. It is also a firm that has experienced strong headwinds recently, since its fate is largely tied to macro-economic variables. This adds an interesting dimension to the firm's disclosure environment. As we will see, one of the end goals of analyzing a firm is making a prediction of where the firm is going and what its future financial results will be. Studying a firm that is facing a difficult economic environment and considerable uncertainty will illustrate the issues and difficulties in constructing a set of pro forma Financial Statements. Pro forma statements are essentially forecasted Financial Statements, based upon a thorough analysis of a firm's past results, coupled with prospective statements that management may offer in its 10-K and elsewhere.

We recognize that we will be considering only this one firm and its disclosures made in the U.S. Notwithstanding our narrow focus, most international reporting environments require similar, but not identical, types of disclosures. The purpose of this introduction is to reveal the types of information that a financial modeler will likely need and the locations of disclosures that can meet those needs.

In the FFAA Handbook, we outlined a procedure that we recommend for conducting an analysis of a firm. We repeat and augment those steps that follow.

OVERVIEW OF STEPS FOR ANALYZING A FIRM

1. Determine the Purpose of the Analysis and Choice of Decision Model

Before commencing an analysis of a firm, being clear about the purpose is important. As we wrote in the FFAA Handbook, the goal is almost always to make some decision about the firm, such as whether to lend to the firm, or to invest in the firm, or perhaps to sell to or buy from the firm. These decisions generally require that we predict a relevant aspect of the firm's future. That is, we want to know where the firm is going, more so than where it has been. Creditors want to predict a firm's ability to pay interest and principal. Investors would like to predict the firm's ability to generate cash flows that can support payments of dividends, as well as new investments in growth opportunities, both of which will likely increase the value of the firm and therefore the stock price. Beyond creditors and investors are numerous other interested parties with varying reasons for studying a firm. For instance, competitors may wish to study the firm's strategy to know if a competitive threat will increase. Customers and vendors would be interested in determining whether the firm would be able to service its products or pay its bills.

2. Gather Relevant Data

Even though the focus of analysis is on a firm's future, it must begin with background information. Such background data will provide context, and context is important for making predictions. For example, if the firm is in an industry that is rapidly growing, we would expect different outcomes about firm performance and risk compared to a firm that is in an industry that is dying due to old technologies or changing consumer patterns. Thus, we need various filings at the SEC, such as the 10-K, which will provide these important contexts. We also need press releases to be able to access more timely information, rather than waiting for the firm to make various filings at the SEC. Firms' websites usually have a link for investors for this purpose.

We recommend obtaining information from the following sources, at a minimum:

a. Form 10-K, Items 1, 1A, 2, 3, and 7 (explained below)

b. CEO's letter to shareholders, from the firm's annual report located on the firm's website

c. Auditor's letter (audit opinion), from the 10-K or annual report

d. Recent news about the firm, as well as information about insider stock transactions

e. Opinions from other professional researchers, such as equity and debt analysts

3. Perform Quantitative and Qualitative Assessments of Data

The relevant data gathered in 2, above, will allow us to analyze a firm's position in its industry. That analysis will be both quantitative and qualitative. Quantitative analysis would include calculation and interpretation of relevant ratios which are benchmarked against a competitor, the industry average, and across time. Such analysis is useful because if we see that a particular performance measure has deteriorated relative to prior periods or relative to a competitor, we would be interested in learning what management plans to do about it, if anything. If we have confidence in management, we might predict improvements; otherwise, in the extreme, we might even predict bankruptcy.

Qualitative analysis may include an assessment of the firm's Strengths, Weaknesses, Opportunities, and Threats, a so-called "SWOT" analysis. SWOT is useful because it combines both an assessment of the firm's current situation (strengths and weaknesses), and it forces us to assess what lies ahead in terms of opportunities and threats.

4. Predict the Relevant Future

Next, we make a prediction about a likely outcome of interest. For example, investors want to predict the firm's future cash generating ability. The cash flows that investors try to predict are called "leveraged free cash flows," which they then discount using a relevant discount rate, called the "equity cost of capital." These discounted cash flows represent an estimate of the firm's value for stockholders and therefore help investors decide whether the firm is "fairly" valued. If the discounted value of leveraged free cash flows (that is, the estimate of the firm's fair value) is lower than the observed value (quoted stock price), then the investor may conclude that the firm is overvalued, in which case the investor would sell the stock, or at least not buy it.

5. Conduct Sensitivity Tests and Make a Decision

The process of analysis and prediction is filled with assumptions and estimates. Therefore, we would want to perform sensitivity tests. Sensitivity tests include changing several assumptions to see if we would still reach the same or similar conclusion about the firm's future. Finally, this whole exercise must end with a decision that is based upon the purpose of the analysis, as outlined in step 1. Hopefully, it will be a good decision. However, in financial analysis there is rarely any instant feedback. We often must be patient to learn our "grade," which only the future will be able to tell us, whenever it arrives.

Our purpose in this book is pedagogical. Thus, we will adopt a general approach that multiple users with different purposes would adopt for Steps 1, 2, and 3. However, in this text, we will not complete Steps 4 and 5. These two remaining steps require a more targeted (and less general) approach and require a more thorough treatment. Regardless, as it is, we already have a full agenda.

We will begin with the Form 10-K filing at the SEC.

ACCESSING AND ANALYZING THE 10-K

To obtain the 10-K, we follow these steps:

1. Go to www.sec.gov

2. Go to "Search for Company Filings"

3. Go to "Company or fund name..."

You can search information collected by the SEC several ways:

- Company or fund name, ticker symbol, CIK (Central Index Key), file number, state, country, or SIC (Standard Industrial Classification)
- Most recent filings
- Full text (past four years)
- Boolean and advanced searching, including addresses
- Key mutual fund disclosures
- Mutual fund voting records
- Mutual fund name, ticker, or SEC key (since Feb. 2006)
- Variable insurance products (since Feb. 2006)

4. Go to "CIK or Ticker Symbol," and type in the stock "ticker symbol" for Lowe's, which is LOW. (Note to find a firm's ticker symbol, we can go to www.finance.google.com and begin typing in the firm's name in the "get quotes" box, and the ticker symbol will appear.)

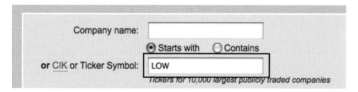

5. Go to "Filing Type." We want Form 10-K, which is the name of the annual filing that contains the Financial Statements, the note disclosures, and other financial information. We type in 10-K here.

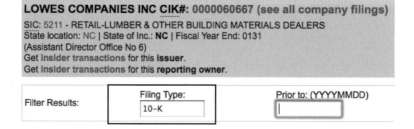

6. *Choose the most recent 10-K, which will be the first one listed, by clicking on the corresponding "Documents" link.*

Filings	Format	Description	Filing Date	File/Film Number
10-K	Documents	Annual report [Section 13 and 15(d), not S-K Item 405] Acc-no: 0000060667-09-000036 (34 Act) Size: 3 MB	2009-03-31	001-07898 07744081
10-K	Documents	Annual report [Section 13 and 15(d), not S-K Item 405] Acc-no: 0000060667-08-000067 (34 Act) Size: 2 MB	2008-04-01	001-07898 061117457
10-K	Documents	Annual report [Section 13 and 15(d), not S-K Item 405] Acc-no: 0000060667-07-000052 (34 Act) Size: 2 MB	2007-04-03	001-07898 06746355

7. *The 10-K is sometimes broken apart into subdocuments, called "Sequences" and abbreviated "Seq." Let's start with Seq 1. From Step #6 we have chosen the most recent 10-K as of and for the annual periods ended January 30, 2009 (we later know this to be Lowe's "2008" filing because most of the covered period was in calendar 2008 despite the fact that is was finalized in 2009).*

Document Format Files

Seq	Description	Document
1	LOWE'S FORM 10-K JANUARY 30, 2009	lowesform10k01302009.htm
2	EXHIBIT 10.10 - AMENDED AND RESTATED LOWE'S COMPANIES, INC. EMPLOYEE STOCK PURCH	exhibit1010.htm
3	EXHIBIT 10.22 - AMENDMENT NUMBER TWO TO THE LOWE'S COMPANIES, INC. DEFERRED COMP	exhibit1022.htm
4	EXHIBIT 10.23 - AMENDMENT NUMBER ONE TO THE LOWE'S COMPANIES, INC. 2006 LONG TER	exhibit1023.htm
5	EXHIBIT 12.1 - STATEMENT RE COMPUTATION OF RATIO OF EARNINGS TO FIXED CHARGES	exhibit121.htm
6	EXHIBIT 13 - PORTIONS OF LOWE'S 2008 ANNUAL REPORT TO SHAREHOLDERS	exhibit13.htm
7	EXHIBIT 21 - LIST OF SUBSIDIARIES	exhibit21.htm
8	EXHIBIT 23 - CONSENT OF DELOITTE & TOUCHE LLP	exhibit23.htm
9	EXHIBIT 31.1 - SECTION 302 CERTIFICATION	exhibit311.htm
10	EXHIBIT 31.2 - SECTION 302 CERTIFICATION	exhibit312.htm
11	EXHIBIT 32.1 - SECTION 906 CERTIFICATION	exhibit321.htm
12	EXHIBIT 32.2 - SECTION 906 CERTIFICATION	exhibit322.htm
13	LOWE'S LOGO	lowesgraphicimage.jpg
	Complete submission text file	0000060667-09-000036.txt

If we scroll down Seq 1, we will see the following Index, listing the various "Items" of the 10-K.

Source: Lowe's 2008 10-K

LOWE'S COMPANIES, INC.
- INDEX -

PART I

Item 1. Business

Item 1A. Risk Factors

Item 1B. Unresolved Staff Comments

Item 2. Properties

Item 3. Legal Proceedings

Item 4. Submission of Matters to a Vote of Security Holders

Executive Officers of the Registrant

PART II

Item 5. Market for Registrant's Common Equity, Related Stockholder Matters and Issuer Purchases of Equity Securities

Item 6. Selected Financial Data

Item 7. Management's Discussion and Analysis of Financial Condition and Results of Operations

Item 7A. Quantitative and Qualitative Disclosures About Market Risk

Item 8. Financial Statements and Supplementary Data

Item 9. Changes in and Disagreements with Accountants on Accounting and Financial Disclosure

Item 9A. Controls and Procedures

Item 9B. Other Information

PART III

Item 10. Directors, Executive Officers and Corporate Governance

Item 11. Executive Compensation

Item 12. Security Ownership of Certain Beneficial Owners and Management and Related Stockholder Matters

Item 13. Certain Relationships and Related Transactions, and Director Independence

Item 14. Principal Accounting Fees and Services

PART IV

Item 15. Exhibits, Financial Statement Schedules

Signatures

Contained in the current document (Seq 1), we have Items 1 – 5, with most of the remaining items (Items 6 – 15) being cross referenced to other documents. We will not consider all of the items. Rather, we will concentrate on those that are generally considered most important. In particular, we will look briefly at Items 1, 1A, 2, and 3. Later we will go to another document to introduce Item 7, and then we will analyze Lowe's Financial Statements and the accompanying note disclosures.

Items 1 and 1A of the 10-K: Business and Risk Factors
Item 1 contains a description of the business. This is useful in learning about the industry and the firm's position in the industry. We learn what products the firm sells, where the products come from, the number of employees, the size of the market for the firm's products, etc. We often can infer the firm's strategy from reading this section as well. Item 1A contains some general risk factors. When we try to assess a firm's future, we are focused on the firm's future performance and risk, so this section can be useful in helping us consider events that are associated with Lowe's risk. Excerpts of Lowe's Items 1 and 1A are below. We do not include the entire Items but have pulled a representative sample of the kinds of information found in these Items.

SOURCE: LOWE'S 2008 10-K
Item 1 – Business

GENERAL INFORMATION

Lowe's Companies, Inc. and subsidiaries (the Company) is a Fortune 50 company and the world's second largest home improvement retailer. As of January 30, 2009, we operated 1,638 stores across 50 states and 11 stores in Canada. Our 1,649 stores represent approximately 187 million square feet of retail selling space.

Incorporated in North Carolina in 1952, Lowe's Companies, Inc. has been publicly held since 1961. Our common stock is listed on the New York Stock Exchange—ticker symbol "LOW."

WHO WE SERVE

We serve homeowners, renters and Commercial Business Customers. Homeowners and renters primarily consist of do-it-yourself (DIY) customers and do-it-for-me (DIFM) customers who utilize our installed sales programs, as well as others buying for personal and family use. Commercial Business Customers include those who work in the construction, repair/remodel, commercial and residential property management, and business maintenance professions.

To meet customers' varying home improvement needs, we offer a complete line of products and services for home decorating, maintenance, repair, remodeling, and property maintenance. We offer home improvement products in the following categories: appliances, lumber, paint, flooring, building materials, millwork, lawn & landscape products, fashion plumbing, hardware, lighting, tools, seasonal living, rough plumbing, outdoor power equipment, cabinets & countertops, nursery, rough electrical, home environment, home organization, and windows & walls.

OUR MARKET

Using the most recent comprehensive data available, which is from 2007, we estimate the size of the U.S. home improvement market to be approximately $695 billion annually, comprised of $535 billion of product demand and $160 billion of installed labor opportunity during that period. Data from a variety of primary and secondary sources, including trade associations, government publications, industry participants and other sources was analyzed as the basis for our estimate. This data captures a wide range of categories relevant to our business, including major appliances and garden supplies. Based on the most recently available data we believe that the size of the U.S. home improvement market decreased by more than 7% in 2008.

The home improvement retailing business includes many competitors. We compete with a number of traditional hardware, plumbing, electrical and home supply retailers, as well as other chains of warehouse home improvement stores and lumberyards in most of our trade areas. In addition, we compete, with respect to some of our products, with general merchandise stores, mail order firms, warehouse clubs, and online retailers. The principal competitive factors are customer service, location, price, product and brand selection, and name recognition.

There are many variables that impact consumer demand for the products and services we offer. Key indicators we monitor include employment, real disposable personal income, housing turnover, and home ownership levels. We also monitor demographic and societal trends that are indicators of home improvement industry growth.

Employment is an indicator of home improvement sales. The forecasted average unemployment rate of 8.6% for 2009 from the March 2009 Blue Chip Economic Indicators™ is higher than the 5.7% average seen in 2008 and suggests that Americans will continue to face challenging employment prospects this year.

Although real disposable personal income continues to grow, it is projected to grow at a slower pace for 2009 than the long-term average annual increase of 3.4%, calculated from 1960 to 2008. Real disposable personal income growth is forecasted to be 1.7% for calendar 2009, compared with 1.1% for calendar 2008, based on data from the March 2009 Blue Chip Economic Indicators™.

Housing turnover, which peaked in calendar year 2005, continues to slow according to The National Association of Realtors®. Recent data suggests that 2009 will remain challenging for housing turnover.

According to the U.S. Census Bureau, while U.S. home ownership levels over the past year have continued their decline from 2007, they remain above their historical average. Home ownership provides an established customer base for home maintenance and repair projects. The vast majority of our customers are homeowners and they are not willing to let what is often their most valuable financial asset deteriorate.

Currently, all of these indicators suggest continued weakness in consumer demand. In this economic environment, we seek to balance our long-term growth plans with a near-term focus on conserving capital and maintaining liquidity.

OUR PRODUCTS

Product Sourcing

We source our products from over 7,000 merchandise vendors worldwide, with no single vendor accounting for more than seven percent of total purchases. Management believes that alternative and competitive suppliers are available for virtually all our products. Whenever possible, we purchase directly from manufacturers to provide savings for our customers and gross margin improvement for Lowe's.

In addition to offering a wide selection of national brand name merchandise, we are committed to building long-term value for Lowe's through the development of exclusive, proprietary brands where we focus on delivering the best quality, the best value and recognizably differentiated products to meet our customers' needs and wants.

National Brand Name Merchandise

In many product categories, customers look for a brand they know and trust to instill confidence in their purchase. A typical Lowe's home improvement store stocks approximately 40,000 items, with hundreds of thousands of items available through our Special Order Sales system. Each store carries a wide selection of national brand name merchandise such as KitchenAid®, Samsung, Whirlpool®, Pella®, Werner®, Kohler®, DeWalt®, John Deere, Troy-Bilt®, Bosch®, Valspar®, Owens Corning®, Electrolux®, Porter-Cable® and many more. Our merchandise selection provides the DIY, DIFM and Commercial Business Customer a one-stop shop for products needed to complete home improvement, repair, maintenance or construction projects.

Proprietary Brands

To further differentiate our offering, we carry many brands that are exclusive to Lowe's. These unique brands cover several categories like lighting, flooring, tools and more, and give our customers great quality and value. Exclusive brand names such as Premier Living™, Kobalt®, Portfolio®, Harbor Breeze®, Reliabilt®, Top-Choice® Lumber and Utilitech™ are found only at Lowe's.

Team Lowe's Racing

NASCAR remains an important part of building our brand. We are the proud sponsor of Jimmie Johnson, three time NASCAR Sprint® Cup Series champion, the #48 car and Lowe's Motor Speedway. We also host hospitality events at various sites throughout the racing season, leveraging and further building membership in the Team Lowe's Racing Fan Club. In 2008, we continued to sponsor Adrian Fernandez and Fernandez Racing to field the #15 car in the American Le Mans Series whose fan base is very different than that of NASCAR. Going to market through both the #48 and #15 teams, helps us to connect with a broad base of customers through one of America's favorite sports – auto racing.

EMPLOYEES

As of January 30, 2009, we employed approximately 164,000 full-time and 65,000 part-time employees, none of which are covered by collective bargaining agreements. Management considers its relations with its employees to be good.

Item 1A - Risk Factors

We are exposed to a variety of risks and uncertainties. Most are general risks and uncertainties applicable to all retailers, but some are more particular to retailers serving the home improvement industry. Our operations may also be affected by factors that are either not currently known to us or which we currently consider immaterial to our business. We describe below some of the specific known factors that could negatively affect our business, financial condition and results of operations. All forward-looking statements made by us in this Annual Report to the Securities and Exchange Commission on Form 10-K, in our Annual Report to Shareholders and in our subsequently filed quarterly and current reports to the Securities and Exchange Commission, as well as in our press releases and other public communications, are qualified by the risks described below.

Our sales are dependent upon the health and stability of the general economy. General economic factors and other conditions, both domestically and internationally, may adversely affect the U.S. economy, the global economy and our financial performance. These include, but are not limited to, periods of flat economic growth or recession, volatility and/or lack of liquidity from time to time in U.S. and world financial markets and the consequent reduced availability and/ or higher cost of credit to Lowe's and its customers, slower rates of growth in real disposable personal income, higher rates of unemployment, higher consumer debt levels, increasing fuel and energy costs, inflation or deflation of commodity prices, natural disasters, acts of terrorism and developments in the war against terrorism in Asia and the Middle East.

The deep global recession that officially began in the U.S. in December 2007 and the financial/credit crisis that has led to the collapse, government bailout or acquisition of weakened major financial institutions have had and will continue to have significant adverse effects on our results of operations. Rising unemployment, reduced consumer confidence and reduced access to credit have combined to lead to sharply reduced consumer spending, particularly by our customers on many of the discretionary, big-ticket items we sell that tend to be larger home improvement project driven. Consumer confidence and willingness to spend on discretionary items remains low and our sales and results of operations will continue to be adversely affected throughout the current fiscal year and, if the recovery from this deep recessionary period and financial crisis is unusually gradual and prolonged as some are predicting, potentially beyond."

What are a few of the key points from the above excerpt? Lowe's sources products from over 7,000 vendors. Should one of these go out of business, others could apparently fill the void. The market is highly fragmented, meaning that many of Lowe's products can be found in other retail outlets. This means that Lowe's must price its products competitively, or else it is quite easy for customers to go elsewhere for the same product at a cheaper price. Notwithstanding fragmentation, Lowe's commands about 7% of the overall estimated market, based upon revenues. Lowe's revenues are close to $50 billion and the overall market is estimated (for product and services combined) to be about $700 billion (7%=50/700). This statistic may suggest that Lowe's has tremendous purchasing power, since it can buy large quantities of inventories and thereby put pressure on vendors to provide low pricing in exchange for large orders.

Lowe's indicates that its fate is tied to employment levels, home ownership levels, housing turnover, and other macro-variables. Given the current environment, Lowe's hints at a strategy in the following statements, copied from above:

Currently, all of these indicators suggest continued weakness in consumer demand. In this economic environment, we seek to balance our long-term growth plans with a near-term focus on conserving capital and maintaining liquidity.

We expect growth therefore to continue (that is, we expect Lowe's to continue to open new stores in new markets) but perhaps at a slower rate, allowing the firm to conserve capital and maintain liquidity. When and if these macro-economic variables improve, Lowe's will have the financial flexibility and liquidity needed to take advantage of the turnaround and accelerate its growth efforts.

Now let's look at Item 2 of the 10-K.

Item 2 of the 10-K: Properties

Item 2 discusses the nature, size, and location of the firm's physical properties. If a large portion of the properties are in areas exposed to particular types of risk (political, expropriation, weather-related, etc.) it is a good for investors to know.

Item 2 – Properties

At January 30, 2009 we operated 1,649 stores in the U.S. and Canada with a total of 187 million square feet of selling space. Of the total stores operating at January 30, 2009, approximately 88% are owned, which includes stores on leased land, with the remainder being leased from unaffiliated third-parties. Approximately 49% of our store leases are capital leases. We also own and operate 14 RDCs and 13 FDCs for lumber and building commodities. We lease and operate two additional FDCs. We operate one third-party distribution facility to serve our Canadian stores. We also operate four facilities to support our import business, Special Order Sales and internet fulfillment. We own two and lease two of these facilities. In addition, we utilize three third-party transload facilities, which do not hold inventory but are the first point of receipt for imported products. We own one data center and lease one data center that serve as hubs for our computer processing, critical data storage and information technology systems. We own our executive offices, which are located in Mooresville, North Carolina. We also own and maintain offices in Wilkes County, North Carolina, and lease and maintain offices in Toronto, Canada and Monterrey, Mexico.

We see that Lowe's appears to prefer to own its properties, rather than lease them. Ownership has certain advantages. If property values increase, Lowe's will benefit from owning the properties, should it decide to sell them. Of course, the reverse is also true, so there are certain risks, as well as potential benefits of ownership. If Lowe's decides to exit a particular area and try to sell the property, it may have to sell it at a loss. Instead, if Lowe's leased the property, it may have to pay lease cancellation penalties, but these could be less than the loss on the sale of the property. Typically, leasing adds a degree of flexibility to entering and exiting markets, compared to owning. (By the way, RDCs and FDCs are regional and flatbed distribution centers, respectively.) As far as any potential risks associated with its properties, we see that most are U.S. and Canadian-based. Risks would be minimal.

Now let's move to Item 3.

Item 3 of the 10-K: Legal Proceedings

Item 3 contains information about Legal Proceedings. We need to be aware of potential, material losses that the firm may suffer from pending lawsuits. If a firm has many significant legal challenges, these would reflect another source of risk to the firm, since they would represent potential, material cash flows to parties other than lenders and investors. Lowe's has a relatively "lawsuit-free" environment, as seen in the following excerpt. By contrast, firms such as pharmaceuticals have multiple descriptions of legal challenges.

Item 3 – Legal Proceedings

We are a defendant in legal proceedings considered to be in the normal course of business, none of which, individually or collectively, is considered material.

Let's now turn to the Financial Statements. The Financial Statements are in Seq 6, "exhibit13.htm." It is not unusual to find the Financial Statements in a separate file, although sometimes they are in the same file (Seq 1). We need to "back up" to the previous page, shown below, and select Seq 6.

Document Format Files

Seq	Description	Document
1	LOWE'S FORM 10-K JANUARY 30, 2009	lowesform10k01302009.htm
2	EXHIBIT 10.10 - AMENDED AND RESTATED LOWE'S COMPANIES, INC. EMPLOYEE STOCK PURCH	exhibit1010.htm
3	EXHIBIT 10.22 - AMENDMENT NUMBER TWO TO THE LOWE'S COMPANIES, INC. DEFERRED COMP	exhibit1022.htm
4	EXHIBIT 10.23 - AMENDMENT NUMBER ONE TO THE LOWE'S COMPANIES, INC. 2006 LONG TER	exhibit1023.htm
5	EXHIBIT 12.1 - STATEMENT RE COMPUTATION OF RATIO OF EARNINGS TO FIXED CHARGES	exhibit121.htm
6	EXHIBIT 13 - PORTIONS OF LOWE'S 2008 ANNUAL REPORT TO SHAREHOLDERS	exhibit13.htm
7	EXHIBIT 21 - LIST OF SUBSIDIARIES	exhibit21.htm
8	EXHIBIT 23 - CONSENT OF DELOITTE & TOUCHE LLP	exhibit23.htm
9	EXHIBIT 31.1 - SECTION 302 CERTIFICATION	exhibit311.htm
10	EXHIBIT 31.2 - SECTION 302 CERTIFICATION	exhibit312.htm
11	EXHIBIT 32.1 - SECTION 906 CERTIFICATION	exhibit321.htm
12	EXHIBIT 32.2 - SECTION 906 CERTIFICATION	exhibit322.htm
13	LOWE'S LOGO	lowesgraphicimage.jpg
	Complete submission text file	0000060667-09-000036.txt

In Exhibit13, we see that Item 7 is first. This is one of the most important Items of the 10-K. It is called ◄**Management Discussion and Analysis (MD&A)**►. The MD&A describes the Financial Statements from management's perspective. However, we will first look at the Financial Statements ourselves and then backtrack to see what management has to say about its Financial Statements. This is a more efficient approach.

We begin with Lowe's Income Statement. Commentary follows. Much of the commentary will reference and reinforce the materials covered in the FFAA Handbook.

Lowe's Income Statement						
Fiscal years ended on	January 30, 2009	%	February 1, 2008	%	February 2, 2007	%
Net sales (Note 1)	48,230	100	48,283	100	46,927	100
Cost of sales (Note 1)	31,729	65.79	31,556	65.36	30,729	65.48
Gross margin	16,501	34.21	16,727	34.64	16,198	34.52
Expenses:						
Selling, general and administrative (Notes 1, 3, 6, 8, 9 and 12)	11,074	22.96	10,515	21.78	9,738	20.75
Store opening costs (Note 1)	102	0.21	141	0.29	146	0.31
Depreciation (Notes 1 and 4)	1,539	3.19	1,366	2.83	1,162	2.48
Interest – net (Notes 10 and 15)	280	0.58	194	0.4	154	0.33

Fiscal years ended on	January 30, 2009	%	February 1, 2008	%	February 2, 2007	%
Total expenses	**12,995**	**26.9**	**12,216**	**25.3**	**11,200**	**23.87**
Pre-tax earnings	**3,506**	**7.27**	**4,511**	**9.34**	**4,998**	**10.65**
Income tax provision (Note 10)	1,311	2.72	1,702	3.52	1,893	4.03
Net earnings	**2,195**	**4.55**	**2,809**	**5.82**	**3,105**	**6.62**
Basic earnings per share (Note 11)	1.51		1.9		2.02	
Diluted earnings per share (Note 11)	1.49		1.86		1.99	
Cash Dividends per share	0.335		0.29		0.18	

Notice how the dates of the Income Statements vary from year to year by a day or two. We learn from Note 1, also in the same document, that Lowe's fiscal year-end (FYE) "is the Friday nearest the end of January." Many retailers have their FYE at the end of January (or the beginning of February) to avoid the busy holiday shopping season. FYE is when firms "close" their books for the year.

Also notice that U.S. firms are required to give three comparative Income Statements. They also must give three comparative Cash Flow Statements, but, as we will see below, only two Balance Sheets.

We see next to several Income Statement accounts that there are references to "Notes". These are the note disclosures discussed in the FFAA Handbook. For example, SG&A Expense references 6 different Notes. The note disclosures often give details about the accounts and the accounting treatment that a firm uses.

Lowe's had $48,230 million (or $48.23 billion) in revenues for the most recent fiscal period, down slightly from the previous year. It is important that we understand a firm's revenue recognition policy. We recall from the FFAA Handbook that under the Revenue Principle, firms generally recognize revenue when it is earned and realized or realizable. "Earned" means that the firm has largely completed the service or shipped the goods. "Realized" means that the firm got paid, and "realizable" means that the firm is likely to be paid.

Firms must provide note disclosures about how they specifically implement the Revenue Principle, as well as other applicable accounting principles. Most of these types of disclosures are found in Note 1, which is usually titled, "Summary of Significant Accounting Policies."

Below are excerpts from Lowe's note disclosure on its revenue recognition policy:

> The Company recognizes revenues...when sales transactions occur and customers take possession of the merchandise.
>
> Revenues from product installation services are recognized when the installation is completed.
>
> Deferred revenues associated with amounts received for which customers have not yet taken possession of merchandise or for which installation has not yet been completed were $328 million and $332 million at January 30, 2009, and February 1, 2008, respectively.
>
> Revenues from stored value cards, which include gift cards and returned merchandise credits, are deferred and recognized when the cards are redeemed. The liability associated with outstanding stored value cards was $346 million and $385 million at

January 30, 2009, and February 1, 2008, respectively, and these amounts are included in deferred revenue on the consolidated balance sheets.

Lowe's sells separately-priced extended warranty contracts under a Lowe's-branded program for which the Company is ultimately self-insured. The Company recognizes revenue from extended warranty sales on a straight-line basis over the respective contract term. Extended warranty contract terms primarily range from one to four years from the date of purchase or the end of the manufacturer's warranty, as applicable. The Company's extended warranty deferred revenue is included in other liabilities (non-current) on the consolidated balance sheets.

As we see, Lowe's records sales of inventory upon shipment (that is, when the customer pays with cash or credit and walks out the door with the inventory). Service revenue is booked upon completion of the service. Lowe's has deferred revenues from customer advance payments, both for products and services. Lowe's also has deferred revenues for gift cards. When someone buys a gift card, Lowe's receives cash and sets up the liability for deferred revenues. The revenue from the gift cards will be recognized when the gift card is used (redeemed). By way of review, we show how deferred revenues affect the fundamental accounting equation, first upon receipt of $100 of cash (assumed), then redemption of the gift card.

Assets		Liabilities		Owners' Equity	
+ 100	Cash	+ 100	Deferred Revenue		

Assets		Liabilities		Owners' Equity	
		- 100	Deferred Revenue	+ 100	Revenue

Lowe's also has deferred revenues from extended warranties. When a customer buys a product (for example a refrigerator), Lowe's will offer an extended warranty, or a warranty that extends the manufacturer's warranty that comes with the refrigerator. Suppose that the manufacturer's warranty covers defects for one year, but Lowe's extended warranty will add another 4 years of coverage. When Lowe's receives cash from the customer for the extended warranty, it must initially offset the cash as "deferred revenue." As time passes on the warranty, Lowe's can then reduce deferred revenues and increase Owners' Equity for revenues.

In Note 1, Lowe's provides the following additional information about its extended warranties.

(In millions)		2008		2007
Extended warranty deferred revenue, beginning of year	$	407	$	315
Additions to deferred revenue		193		175
Deferred revenue recognized		(121)		(83)
Extended warranty deferred revenue, end of year	$	479	$	407

Thus, we can re-create Lowe's journal entries, which we do below.

Assets		Liabilities		Owners' Equity	
+ 193	Cash	+ 193	Deferred Revenues		

Assets		Liabilities		Owners' Equity	
		- 121	Deferred Revenues	+ 121	Revenues

The important point is that we need to read a firm's Summary of Significant Accounting Policies and make sure that the application of accounting principles for the particular firm that we are studying makes sense. If an application of accounting principles seems unusual, we should try to learn more about the accounting principle and the accounting practices in that firm's industry. One way to do this is to read the Summary of Significant Accounting Policies of other firms in the industry. If our firm of interest is applying principles in unusual ways, we should try to understand if the business model justifies deviations from the normal practices. If we are still unable to feel comfortable with the firm's application of accounting principles, then perhaps we should beware of the firm under consideration. In the case of Lowe's, nothing appears to be out of the ordinary for a firm in the retail sector.

Continuing on the Income Statement, as a convenience (but not a requirement) Lowe's provides ◀**common size ratios**▶. To calculate common size ratios for Income Statement accounts, each account is divided by Net Sales. This facilitates a comparison of Lowe's results to other firms (of a different absolute size) and a comparison of Lowe's results in one year to those of prior years.

For instance, Cost of Sales (which is another name for Cost of Goods Sold, COGS) was $31,729. On a common size basis, Cost of Sales is 65.79% ($31,729/48,230), which is higher than the previous year (65.36% = 31,556/48,283).

A related ratio is the Gross Margin. Gross Margin is: (Sales – COGS) / Sales.

As Lowe's discloses on the Income Statement, its Gross Margin fell from 34.64% to 34.21% over the most recent year. One explanation could be that Lowe's had to lower selling prices to generate sales. Gross Margins may remain under pressure in the tough economy, as Lowe's may have to reduce selling prices further.

As we can see, the Cost Ratio and the Gross Margin add to 1. For example, for the most recent year:

Cost Ratio	+	**Gross Margin**	= 1
65.79%	+	34.21%	= 1

More generally, this can be seen in the following "proof:"

Cost Ratio	+	**Gross Margin**	= 1
COGS / Sales	+	(Sales – COGS) / Sales	= 1
COGS / Sales	+	Sales / Sales – COGS / Sales	= 1
Sales	/	Sales	= 1

Cost of Sales is often a mixture of several different cost categories. It is sort of like a "soup" with many different ingredients. To find all of the items included in Lowe's Cost of Sales, we can go to the note disclosures. Lowe's includes all of the following in its Cost of Sales:

- Purchase costs, net of vendor funds;
- Freight expenses associated with moving merchandise inventories from vendors to retail stores;
- Costs associated with operating the Company's distribution network, including payroll and benefit costs and occupancy costs;
- Costs of installation services provided;
- Costs associated with delivery of products directly from vendors to customers by third parties

The above costs reveal that some items, which we would traditionally consider to be expensed, were actually capitalized as part of inventory first, and then expensed (as COGS) when the inventory was sold. For instance, we note that payroll and shipping costs were capitalized as part of inventory, whereas we typically see these items as immediately being part of SG&A Expense. The reason these costs are capitalized is the Cost Principle, discussed in the FFAA Handbook. All costs necessary to bring the asset (inventory, in this case) to its place of intended use or sale are capitalized as part of inventory.

Continuing on the Income Statement, we see that SG&A Expense has grown from 21.78% of sales in the previous year to 22.96% (11,074/48,230) in the most recent year. SG&A Expense is commonly referred to as "Operating Expenses" and include items such as rent, insurance, wages (other than those mentioned above as part of COGS), and salaries. SG&A Expense is another "soup." Similar to COGS, the components of SG&A Expense are provided as note disclosures. For Lowe's, SG&A Expense includes the following:

- Payroll and benefit costs for retail and corporate employees;
- Occupancy costs of retail and corporate facilities;
- Advertising;
- Costs associated with delivery of products from stores to customers;
- Third-party, in-store service costs;
- Tender costs, including bank charges, costs associated with credit card interchange fees and amounts associated with accepting the Company's proprietary credit cards;
- Costs associated with self-insured plans, and premium costs for stop-loss coverage and fully insured plans;
- Long-lived asset impairment charges and gains/losses on disposal of assets;
- Other administrative costs, such as supplies, and travel and entertainment.

Payroll, occupancy (such as rent), advertising and a few other expenses included in SG&A Expense are typical components. We often can find more details on the amounts of these components elsewhere in the notes. For example, Lowe's reports in Note 1 that advertising expenses were as follows:

Advertising – Costs associated with advertising are charged to expense as incurred. Advertising expenses were $789 million, $788 million and $873 million in 2008, 2007 and 2006, respectively.

The less typical components of SG&A Expense are the asset impairment charges and gains and losses on asset disposals. These are often considered ‹**non-recurring items**›, but Lowe's includes them as part of Operating Expenses, indicating that these types of items occur regularly in Lowe's operating environment. Lowe's owns large amounts of physical assets, primarily buildings and property for its retail stores. Lowe's is constantly reassessing the profitability of the investments in these properties. Such reassessment is a normal part of its business and will lead to the conclusions that certain assets are impaired and some should be sold altogether.

As we described in the FFAA Handbook, asset impairments vary by asset category and by accounting regimes, but the general notion is that the asset in question has lost value and is shown on the Balance Sheet at a book value that is higher than its fair value. Generally, the asset must be "written down" in these circumstances. Lowe's describes impairments in its Summary of Significant Accounting Policies (Note 1 of the 10-K):

> The carrying amounts of long-lived assets are reviewed whenever events or changes in circumstances indicate that the carrying amount may not be recoverable.
>
> The charge for impairment is included in SG&A expense. The Company recorded long-lived asset impairment charges of $21 million during 2008, including $16 million for operating stores and $5 million for relocated stores, closed stores and other excess properties.

The impairment would have been recorded as follows:

Assets		Liabilities		Owners' Equity	
(21)	Assets			(21)	SG&A Expense

Also in Note 1, Lowe's has the following description of asset dispositions:

> Upon disposal, the cost of properties and related accumulated depreciation are removed from the accounts, with gains and losses reflected in SG&A expense on the consolidated statements of earnings.

Finally, we also note that Lowe's discloses that it has investments that are classified as "Trading" securities. As we introduced in the FFAA Handbook, Trading securities are marked-to-market, with unrealized gains and losses reported in the Income Statement. Lowe's includes these unrealized gains and losses as part of SG&A Expense, as is discloses in Note 1:

> The Company maintains investment securities in conjunction with certain employee benefit plans that are classified as trading securities. These securities are carried at fair market value with unrealized gains and losses included in SG&A expense.

The main point of our extended analysis of SG&A Expense is to illustrate how many different ingredients are in the soup. This is important to recognize for the following reason. We normally consider SG&A Expense to be a variable expense, meaning that it varies with sales. However, it will not vary directly with sales because of all of the items included in SG&A Expense that are completely unrelated to sales. Thus, in modeling SG&A Expense for the ensuing year, we would not necessarily expect that SG&A Expense would change by exactly the same percentage as that forecasted for sales

We also point out that normally gains and losses are shown as part of the "Non operating Section" of the Income Statement. By putting these gains and losses in SG&A Expense, they show up as part of the Operating Section, or EBIT. If the gains and losses on asset disposals are significant, most firms will break them out as a "line item" on the Income Statement, so readers will see them more clearly. Lowe's is essentially indicating that these gains and losses occur regularly as part of their selling various long-lived assets.

Occasionally, we see cases where firms bury gains inside expense accounts, such as SG&A Expense, to make the expense account appear smaller and to make the firm appear more efficient. Thus, it is a good idea to check SG&A Expense to see all of the items included.

Not shown in the Income Statement are year-over-year ratios. Year-over-year is often abbreviated YOY or Y/Y. These are also useful, in conjunction with common size ratios, to spot recent trends. As mentioned, Net Sales fell slightly over the most recent period:

YOY Sales $\quad\quad = \$48,230 / 48,283 - 1$

$\quad\quad\quad\quad\quad\quad = -0.1\%$

Depreciation Expense, Interest Expense, and SG&A Expense all increased significantly YOY.

YOY Depreciation $\quad = 1,539 / 1,366 - 1$

$\quad\quad\quad\quad\quad\quad = 12.7\%$

YOY Interest $\quad\quad = 280 / 194 - 1$

$\quad\quad\quad\quad\quad\quad = 44.3\%$

YOY SG&A $\quad\quad = 11,074 / 10,515 - 1$

$\quad\quad\quad\quad\quad\quad = 5.3\%$

The above analysis largely explains why Net Income fell. Namely, not only did sales fall, all expense categories rose YOY. YOY Net Income is below:

YOY Net Income $\quad = 2,195 / 2,809 - 1$

$\quad\quad\quad\quad\quad\quad = -21.9\%$

Let's focus momentarily on Depreciation Expense. We see that it amounts to $1,539 million for the most recent year. We also remember from the FFAA Handbook that depreciation is also found on the Statement of Cash Flows. In fact, using the Indirect Method, Depreciation Expense and Amortization Expense are typically the first items added back to Net Income. Depreciation Expense and Amortization Expense are non-cash expenses that are subtracted from income but that do not involve cash. Thus, to move from accrual-based Net Income to operating cash flow, we undo the effects of all non-cash charges. So, let's see what the Statement of Cash Flows shows as Depreciation Expense.

Below, we give the beginning portion of Lowe's Statement of Cash Flows. We re-visit the statement shortly and consider the other sections. We see that total Depreciation and Amortization is $1,667, whereas we find only $1,539 on the Income Statement. The difference of $128 million (1,667 – 1,539) is likely included in inventory, and then subsequently becomes part of COGS. As we recall, when we saw the ingredients of the COGS "soup," it included costs associated with the distribution of inventory throughout the system. Thus, it is likely that some portion of the depreciation on the distribution centers is allocated to inventory (that is, "capitalized" in inventory) and then expensed when the inventory is sold.

For the years ended on	January 30, 2009	February 1, 2008	February 2, 2007
Net earnings	2,195	2,809	3,105
Adjustments to reconcile net earnings to net cash provided by operating activities:			
Depreciation and amortization	1,667	1,464	1,237

The important point is that for purposes of financial modeling, we need to find total depreciation and amortization, because we will want to estimate future Statements of Cash Flows. Thus, we need to be able to estimate total non-cash expenses in order to "un-do" their effects on cash flows from operations. In fact, what we often do is remove Depreciation Expense from COGS and include it with the "regular" Depreciation Expense category (below Gross Margin on the Income Statement) to make the modeling clearer. We refer to "depreciation-free" COGS as ◀clean COGS.▶

Another important point with respect to financial modeling is to understand the firm's depreciation policy. Straight-line is the most common method, but it pays to be sure. Lowe's gives the following disclosure in its Summary of Significant Accounting Policies (Note 1 of the 10-K):

> Depreciation is provided over the estimated useful lives of the depreciable assets. Assets are depreciated using the straight-line method.

Below Operating Income, we find "Non-operating Income." Sometimes analysts refer to this as ◀the line▶ that is, the separation between Operating and Non-operating Income. "Above the line" items are part of Operating Income, and "below the line" items are part of Non-operating Income. However, "the line" is not anything official and some analysts place "the line" in slightly different places on the Income Statement. The main point of the demarcation is to highlight those items in the Income Statement that are part of Lowe's central, ongoing operations and therefore more likely to be sustainable or to repeat. Knowing this attribute of various items on the Income Statement is helpful, for fairly clear reasons, in building financial models.

The Non-operating items on Lowe's Income Statement include investing items (such as interest income) and financing related items (such as interest expense). Lowe's reports only one non-operating item: Net Interest Expense ($280 million). The items netted against interest expense are explained in the notes, and include interest income and capitalized interest.

Below is Lowe's note disclosure about its Net Interest Expense (from the 10-K):

(In millions)	2008	2007	2006
Long-term debt	$ 292	$ 247	$ 183
Short-term borrowings	11	8	1
Capitalized leases	31	32	34
Interest income	(40)	(45)	(52)
Interest capitalized	(36)	(65)	(32)
Other	22	17	20
Interest – net	$ 280	$ 194	$ 154

As we see above, $36 million of interest is capitalized in Property, Plant and Equipment. We also note that Lowe's offsets interest expense with interest income, which is not unusual. Lowe's earned interest income of $40 million on various investments. Lowe's gross interest expense, after backing-out the effect of interest income and interest capitalized, is $356 ($280 + 40 + 36).

It is important to "un-do" the netting of interest income and capitalized interest against interest expense. For instance, the Effective Interest Rate is sometimes calculated as total interest expense divided by average interest bearing debt. If net interest expense is used, then the Effective Interest Rate would be understated. (There are other ways to estimate the Effective Interest Rate which we did not cover in the FFAA Handbook.) The Effective Interest Rate is used in several other ratios, such as the "weighted average cost of capital" which we also did not cover. The important point is that there are often cascading effects on other ratios when one is measured inappropriately.

Next on the Income Statement is "Income Tax Provision." This is another way firms describe Income Tax Expense.

For Lowe's this amounted to $1,311 million (or, $1.311 billion).

Let's calculate Lowe's Effective Tax Rate.

Effective Tax Rate	**= Tax Expense / Pre-Tax Income**
	= 1,311 / 3,506
	= 37.4%

There is a table in the note disclosures that gives the Effective Tax Rate and reconciles the Effective Tax Rate with the Statutory Rate. Lowe's reconciliation is below (from Note 10 in the 10-K). We can see that the primary reason that the Effective Tax Rate for Lowe's is higher than the Statutory Rate is the presence of state income taxes. Our main focus is on the rate itself (37.4%) and whether this rate appears to be fairly steady from year to year:

	2008	2007	2006
Statutory federal income tax rate	35.0%	35.0%	35.0%
State income taxes, net of federal tax benefit	2.9	3.0	3.3
Other, net	(0.5)	(0.3)	(0.4)
Effective tax rate	**37.4%**	**37.7%**	**37.9%**

The Effective Tax Rate is easy to calculate as per the above formula, but the table is useful because it gives the reason for the difference between the two rates. Knowing the reason helps the finance professional determine how likely the rate is to hold steady going forward and professionals need this rate for their financial models. In the case of Lowe's, the rate is fairly steady (trending slightly lower), and since Lowe's will continue to operate largely in the U.S. and be subject to state income taxes, this rate is likely to persist in this range. To assist users, sometimes firms will actually provide expected Effective Tax Rates. If they do, they usually do so in the conference call with analysts when they announce their fourth quarter earnings.

Returning to Lowe's Income Statement, we see the two EPS measures. **◄Basic EPS►** is essentially earnings, or Net Income, divided by the average number of shares of stock outstanding. Diluted EPS represents an adjustment to Basic EPS. **◄Diluted EPS►** includes the effects of stock options and a few other items. Lowe's Basic and Diluted EPS are $1.51 and $1.49, respectively, for the most recent year.

Sometimes finance professionals are focused on forecasting these EPS measures, which means that they not only must forecast the numerators (Net Income and Adjusted Net Income), but also the denominators (average shares outstanding). Predicting the share count means trying to predict both new equity issues and share repurchases. There are several moving parts to this type of "earnings forecast" model, which make forecasting an art, not a science.

Next, we obtain the Balance Sheet:

Lowe's Balance Sheet

Assets	January 30, 2009	%	February 1, 2008	%
Current Assets				
Cash and cash equivalents (Note 1)	245	0.7	281	0.9
Short-term investments (Notes 1, 2 and 3)	416	1.3	249	0.1
Merchandise inventory - net (Note 1)	8,209	25.1	7,611	24.6
Deferred income taxes - net (Notes 1 and 10)	166	0.5	247	0.8
Other current assets (Note 1)	215	0.7	298	0.1
Total Current Assets	**9,251**	**28.3**	**8,686**	**28.1**
Property, less accumulated depreciation (Notes 1 and 4)	22,722	69.5	21,361	69.2
Long-term investments (Notes 1, 2 and 3)	253	0.8	509	1.7
Other assets (Note 1)	460	1.4	313	1.0
Total Assets	**32,686**	**100**	**30,869**	**100**
Liabilities and Shareholders' Equity				
Current Liabilities:				
Short-term borrowings (Note 5)	987	3.0	1,064	3.5
Current maturities of long-term debt (Note 6)	34	0.1	40	0.1
Accounts payable (Note 1)	4,109	12.6	3,713	12.0
Accrued compensation and employee benefits	434	1.3	467	1.5
Self-insurance liabilities (Note 1)	751	2.3	671	2.2
Deferred revenue (Note 1)	674	2.1	717	2.3
Other current liabilities (Note 1)	1,033	3.1	1,079	3.5
Total Current Liabilities	**8,022**	**24.5**	**7,751**	**25.1**
Long-term debt, excluding current maturities (Notes 3, 6 and 12)	5,039	15.4	5,576	18.1
Deferred income taxes - net (Notes 1 and 10)	660	2.0	670	2.2
Other liabilities (Note 1)	910	2.9	774	2.5
Total Liabilities	**14,631**	**44.8**	**14,771**	**47.9**

Commitments and contingencies (Note 13)

	January 30, 2009	%	February 1, 2008	%
Shareholders' Equity (Note 7):				
Preferred stock - $5 par value, none issued	-	-	-	-
Common stock - $.50 par value;				
Shares issued and outstanding				
30-Jan-09 1,470				
1-Feb-08 1,458	735	2.2	729	2.3
Capital in excess of par value	277	0.8	16	0.1
Retained earnings	17,049	52.2	15,345	49.7
Accumulated other comprehensive (loss) income (Note 1)	(6)	-	8	-
Total Shareholders' Equity	**18,055**	**55.2**	**16,098**	**52.1**
Total Liabilities and Shareholders' Equity	**32,686**	**100**	**30,869**	**100**

Let's walk around the Balance Sheet, beginning with cash. Cash includes currency on hand and deposits in checking and savings accounts that can be accessed immediately without penalty. "Cash equivalents" is an unfortunate name, because cash equivalents are not technically equivalent to cash. Cash equivalents are short term investments with an original maturity of 3 months or less. Thus, cash equivalents cannot always be immediately spent without paying some sort of fee (such as a brokerage fee) or a penalty.

Short-term investments are, as the name implies, investments in stocks and bonds that the firm plans to sell within one year. These investments are a way for Lowe's to try to earn a higher return on otherwise idle cash.

Lowe's provides the following note disclosure with respect to its Accounts Receivable (from the 10-K):

> The majority of the Company's accounts receivable arises from sales of goods and services to Commercial Business Customers. The Company has an agreement with General Electric Company and its subsidiaries (GE) under which GE purchases at face value new commercial business accounts receivable originated by the Company and services these accounts.
>
> Sales generated through the Company's proprietary credit cards are not reflected in receivables. Under an agreement with GE, credit is extended directly to customers by GE. All credit-program-related services are performed and controlled directly by GE.

We expect to find Accounts Receivable from firms because they typically make credit sales. However, as we see above, Lowe's sells the receivables in order to speed up cash flow. When we expect to see receivables, but do not find them in the Balance Sheet, we need to verify in the note disclosures that this is what is happening.

Merchandise inventory includes the merchandise that Lowe's sells to customers, such as nails, ladders, plants, lights, appliances, and thousands more such items.

Below is Lowe's inventory disclosure (from the 10-K). Notably, we see that Lowe's uses FIFO:

> Inventory is stated at the lower of cost or market using the first-in, first-out method of inventory accounting. The cost of inventory also includes certain costs associated with the preparation of inventory for resale, including distribution center costs, and is net of vendor funds.

Deferred Tax Assets are future deductions that Lowe's will use to reduce taxes. These are listed as assets because they represent future reductions in the amount of tax that Lowe's would have to pay to the government. In the FFAA Handbook, we described these as deferred deductions, that is, deductions that the firm will be allowed to take, but not on the current tax return, rather on future tax returns. This contrasts with Deferred Tax Liabilities that we describe below. As we mentioned in the FFAA Handbook, Deferred Tax Liabilities result from accelerated deductions. The underlying cause of Lowe's Deferred Tax Assets (i.e., its deferred deductions) stems from Lowe's "Self Insurance Liability," which we address shortly when we cover the various liability accounts.

"Other current assets" is another "soup" (like COGS and SG&A Expense), but this time, this soup is on the Balance Sheet. Note 1 tells us what is included in this account:

> The net carrying value for relocated stores, closed stores and other excess properties that are expected to be sold within the next 12 months is classified as held-for-sale and included in other current assets on the consolidated balance sheets.

As we see, Lowe's indicates that this account contains stores that are "held-for-sale," which are stores that Lowe's has closed and plans to sell within the next 12 months. We need to check the note disclsoures for these types of accounts (both assets and liabilities) that are described as "other." We need to know what is in the account for modeling purposes. If, as in this case, other assets are primarily stores that will be sold, we are better informed about how to forecast future values for this particular account.

Continuing with assets, Lowe's next gives "Property, less accumulated depreciation" of $22,722. This is a "net" amount. The details about the property's total cost and total depreciation are in the below note (Note 4 in the 10-K):

Property is summarized by major class in the following table:

(In millions)	Estimated Depreciable Lives, In Years		January 30, 2009		February 1, 2008
Cost:					
Land	N/A	$	6,144	$	5,566
Buildings	7-40		11,258		10,036
Equipment	3-15		8,797		8,118
Leasehold improvements	5-40		3,576		3,063
Construction in progress	N/A		1,702		2,053
Total cost			31,477		28,836
Accumulated depreciation			(8,755)		(7,475)
Property, less accumulated depreciation		$	2,272	$	21,361

We can see that the property is about one-fourth fully depreciated (8,755/31,477=28%). Also shown above are the ranges of depreciable lives. However, land is not depreciated. Thus the depreciable life is "N/A" (not applicable). Also, "construction in progress" refers to buildings and stores that are currently being built. Firms do not depreciate these buildings until they are completed and placed in service.

We remember that the Cost Principle is applied at the acquisition of these assets. Below are excerpts from Lowe's note disclosure on application of the Cost Principle:

> Property is recorded at cost. Costs associated with major additions are capitalized and depreciated. Capital Assets are expected to yield future benefits and have useful lives which exceed one year. The total cost of a capital asset generally includes all applicable sales taxes, delivery costs, installation costs and other appropriate costs incurred by the Company...

Next, Lowe's shows another amount for investments, but these are long-term investments, whereas the others were short-term. Finally, Lowe's shows "Other assets," which include other closed or relocated stores that Lowe's does not plan to sell in the next 12 months.

On the liability side of the Balance Sheet, Lowe's begins with Short-term borrowings and Current Maturities of Long Term Debt. Both of these represent the principal amounts of loans that the firm will have to repay over the next 12 months. The full repayment schedule of principal beyond the next twelve months is in another note disclosures (Note 6), which we present shortly.

Accounts Payable and Accrued Compensation and Employee Benefits are amounts owed, respectively, to suppliers of inventory and to employees.

Deferred Revenue represents amounts owed to customers. However, what Lowe's owes customers is not cash. Rather, Lowe's owes them either a product or a service. As we saw earlier when we analyzed Lowe's application of the Revenue Principle, Deferred Revenues arose from gift cards and advance payments on products and services. (Deferred Revenues on extended warranties are held in another liability account, discussed below.)

Self Insurance Liability is an estimate of claims for damages that may result from faulty products, injuries, etc. Lowe's must set aside a "reserve" for an estimate of these damages, before any such damages occur. The liability represents a contingent payment to injured parties or for property damage. Lowe's will offset the increase in the liability with a decrease in Owners' Equity. In particular, Lowe's will charge the owners another expense, "insurance expense," which is included in SG&A expense. This is illustrated below with an assumed amount of $100.

Assets		Liabilities		Owners' Equity	
		+ 100	Self Insurance Liability	(100)	SG&A Expense

We remember that Deferred Tax Assets represent future deductions, that is, deductions that Lowe's must defer to future tax periods in accordance with applicable tax law. Next, Lowe's gives (in Note 10 of the 10-K), information about the reasons for its Deferred Tax Assets, and we see that the Self-Insurance Liability is the primary reason.

(In millions)		January 30, 2009	February 1, 2008
Deferred tax assets:			
Self-insurance	$	221 $	189
Share-based payment expense		95	81
Other, net		223	205
Total deferred tax assets	$	**539** $	**475**

Lowe's will be able to deduct the self insurance expense when it has to make actual cash payment to settle insurance claims. Assume for example that a shopper is injured in one of Lowe's stores and Lowe's pays $100 to settle the claim. The entry would be as follows:

Assets		Liabilities		Owners' Equity	
(100)	Cash	(100)	Self Insurance Liability		

When the cash payment is made, Lowe's would likely be able to claim the deduction on its tax return, not when Lowe's initially recorded the SG&A Expense.

Similar to "Other current assets," "Other current liabilities" are described in the note disclosures. Lowe's indicates that these are liabilities to landlords for leases that Lowe's terminates early. These liabilities may represent penalties that Lowe's may have to pay for early termination.

Long term debt represents the principal amount of debt payments that are due beyond one year.

As we see on the Balance Sheet, Lowe's long term debt increased from $4,325 (2006) to $5,576 (2007), but fell to $5,039 in 2008. Reducing debt is referred to as "de-leveraging." As we introduced in the FFAA Handbook, leverage is a concept that refers to the amount of debt in the capital mix. Capital mix is the relative use of debt versus equity. Debt is called ◀leverage▶ because it represents capital that can be put to work on behalf of the owners and thus "lever" (increase) the returns to owners.

The table below gives information about Lowe's debt (from the Lowe's 10-K):

(In millions) Debt Category	Rates	Fiscal Year of Final Maturity	January 30, 2009
Secured debt:[1]			
Mortgage notes	7.00 to 8.25%	2018	27
Unsecured debt:			
Debentures	6.50 to 6.88%	2029	694
Notes	8.25%	2010	500
Medium-term notes - series A	8.19 to 8.20%	2023	15
Medium-term notes - series B2	7.11 to 7.61%	2037	217
Senior notes	5.00 to 6.65%	2037	3,273
Convertible notes			–
Capital leases and other		2030	347
Total long-term debt			**5,073**
Less current maturities			34
Long-term debt, excluding current maturities			**5,039**

Notes and bonds are essentially the same, except for differences in maturities. Lowe's reveals in the below disclosure more details about upcoming maturity dates on their notes (from the 10-K):

> Debt maturities...for the next five years and thereafter are as follows: 2009, $1 million; 2010, $519 million; 2011, $1 million; 2012, $551 million; 2013, $1 million; thereafter, $3.7 billion.

Below is an excerpt that gives more details about one of Lowe's debt issues (from the 10-K):

> In September 2007, the Company issued $1.3 billion of unsecured senior notes, comprised of three tranches: $550 million of 5.60% senior notes maturing in September 2012, $250 million of 6.10% senior notes maturing in September 2017 and $500 million of 6.65% senior notes maturing in September 2037. The 5.60%, 6.10% and 6.65% senior notes were issued at discounts of approximately $2.7 million, $1.3 million and $6.3 million, respectively. Interest on the senior notes is payable semiannually in arrears in March and September of each year until maturity, beginning in March 2008. The discount associated with the issuance is included in long-term debt and is being amortized over the respective terms of the senior notes. The net proceeds of approximately $1.3 billion were used for general corporate purposes, including capital expenditures and working capital needs, and for repurchases of shares of the Company's common stock.

A ‹tranche› is a "slice". The above debt issue of $1.3 billion was sliced into 3 different parts, characterized by different maturity dates (2012, 2017, and 2037) and different stated rates of interest (5.60%, 6.10%, and 6.65%). Typically, longer maturities correspond to higher interest rates to compensate for additional risk associated with the debt holder having to wait so long to be paid back. The notes pay interest every 6 months. Lowe's also reports the reasons for the debt issue (capital expenditures and share repurchases).

Because the tranches were issued at discounts, the market was demanding a somewhat higher return when the debt was issued compared to stated interest rate on the debt.

Next on the Balance Sheet are Deferred Tax Liabilities, which are estimates of future increases of taxes owed to the government, primarily due to the loss of future deductions. That is, firms typically take all allowable deductions early to save taxes in the current period. This means that future tax returns will not have as many deductions, thereby increasing the tax bill. Deferred Tax Liabilities essentially are a consequence of accelerated deductions. This contrasts with Deferred Tax Assets, which, as we saw previously, represent deferred deductions.

Below is an excerpt of Lowe's note disclosure about its Deferred Tax Liabilities (from the 10-K):

(In millions)	January 30, 2009	February 1, 2008
Deferred tax liabilities:		
Property	(977)	(834)
Other, net	(14)	(42)
Total deferred tax liabilities	**(991)**	**(876)**

We can see that the main cause of the firm's Deferred Tax Liability is "Property," but Lowe's does not give further details. We assume that this relates to depreciable property and the difference between accelerated depreciation for tax purposes and straight line depreciation for GAAP purposes.

"Other liabilities," according to the note disclosures, include Deferred Revenue on sales of extended warranties. This Deferred Revenue was discussed earlier and is similar to the Deferred Revenue from gift cards.

We recall from the FFAA Handbook that firms must estimate their contingent liabilities and record those that are probable and estimable. Earlier, we saw in Item 3 of the 10-K that Lowe's is relatively lawsuit-free. Lowe's note disclosure on contingent losses is described more fully below (Note 13 in the 10-K):

> The Company is a defendant in legal proceedings considered to be in the normal course of business, none of which, individually or collectively, are believed to have a risk of having a material impact on the Company's Financial Statements. In evaluating Liabilities associated with its various legal proceedings, the Company has accrued for probable Liabilities associated with these matters. The amounts accrued were not material to the Company's consolidated Financial Statements in any of the years presented.

As we see, Lowe's accrues probable contingent losses. However, Lowe's indicates that the amounts would not have a material adverse effect on the Financial Statements if they must be paid. These accruals for contingent losses are likely included in "Other Liabilities." This is why the space for Commitments and Contingencies on the Balance Sheet is blank, with reference to the above note disclosure.

Turning to Owners' Equity, Lowe's has Common Stock and Capital in Excess of Par Value of $735 and $277, respectively. These amounts primarily represent the amount of money that investors have invested in the firm. We see that the common stock has a so-called ‹par› value of 50 cents. This is a nominal value placed upon a stock certificate that has little meaning today. (It used to represent the minimum amount of capital that investors had to put into a firm, as a protection to creditors.) Par value is intentionally kept very low, because firms generally are not allowed to sell stock below par. If Lowe's were to sell one share of stock for cash at a value of $20, 50 cents would go into the common stock account and $19.50 would go into capital in excess of par value, as shown below:

Assets		Liabilities		Owners' Equity	
+ 20.00	Cash			+ 0.50	Common Stock
				+ 19.50	Capital in Excess of Par Value

Capital in Excess of Par Value is also called Additional Paid in Capital, which is abbreviated APIC.

Retained Earnings are the cumulative earnings of the firm since its inception, less dividends paid to investors. Accumulated Other Comprehensive Income (AOCI) contains various gains and losses that are not included in Retained Earnings. We recall from the FFAA Handbook that investments that the firm classifies as "available-for-sale" are marked-to-market with unrealized gains and losses reported in AOCI, rather than in Net Income. Lowe's has some investments classified in this manner as revealed in the notes:

> All other investment securities are classified as available-for-sale and are carried at fair market value with unrealized gains and losses included in accumulated other comprehensive (loss) income in shareholders' equity.

Similar to the Income Statement, Lowe's also provides common size ratios on the Balance Sheet. To measure common size ratios, each Balance Sheet item is divided by Total Assets. For example, Lowe's common size inventory grew from 24.7% ($7,611 / $30,869) to 25.1% ($8,209 / $32,686) of Total Assets.

As before, not shown are year-over-year (YOY) changes, but we can easily calculate these changes. For example, inventory grew 7.9% from 2007 to 2008.

YOY inventory   = $8,209 / 7,611 − 1

                              = 7.9%

Growing inventory of that magnitude, coupled with declining sales, is usually another cause for concern. This could mean that Gross Margins will continue to be under pressure, because Lowe's may have to reduce selling prices to be able to sell the inventory.

From the above Balance Sheet, let's extract the fundamental equation for the most recent year:

Assets	Liabilities	Owners' Equity
32,686	14,631	18,055

The above equation shows that Lowe's is financed with more Owners' Equity than total Liabilities. We see that the largest part of Owners' Equity is Retained Earnings ($17,049). We sometimes consider Retained Earnings to represent "internally generated equity capital," as opposed to "external equity capital," which would correspond to investments by the owners. This means that Lowe's has been able to finance much of its growth over the years from its own operations.

Assets are broken down into Current and Noncurrent. Current Assets are those that will generally be used, consumed, or sold within one year. Current Liabilities will generally be paid within one year. The Noncurrent categories are simply "not current."

The next level of the fundamental equation for the most recent year is given below:

Assets		Liabilities		Owners' Equity
32,686		14,631		18,055
Current Assets	Noncurrent Assets	Current Liabilities	NonCurrent Liabilities	
9,251	23,435	8,022	6,609	

Lowe's has far more Noncurrent Assets than Current. This is expected given Lowe's large requirement for buildings and real estate for its stores. Lowe's also has somewhat more Current Liabilities than Noncurrent. The Current Liabilities consist primarily of the payables to vendors for inventory.

One disclosure of particular interest for large national retailers, such as Lowe's, is the disclosure about leases. We recall from the FFAA Handbook that most leases are structured in a way to keep them "off-balance-sheet." These leases are operating leases. Firms with operating leases disclose them in the note disclosures.

Below is an excerpt of Lowe's note disclosure about its operating leases (from the 10-K):

(In millions)	Operating Leases
Fiscal Year	
2009	389
2010	389
2011	388
2012	384
2013	379
Later years	4,256
Total minimum lease payments	**6,185**

Firms with operating leases must disclose 5 years of required cash payments (2009 - 2013), and then a lump sum for later years. The lump sum will not be paid as a lump sum, but rather over a period of years. We do not know precisely how long the period of time is. All we know is the $4,256 will be paid over "Later years." The above cash flows are also future cash flows. That is, they are not discounted to present value.

To see how Lowe's Balance Sheet would change if these leases were "on-balance-sheet" (that is, capital leases), we usually will make an adjustment by estimating the present value of the above cash flows and then making an entry to record both the Leased Asset and Lease Liability. One "quick and dirty" shortcut method for capitalizing operating leases is simply to multiply the average lease payment by a factor of about 7.5. The reason is as follows. Many corporate leases have 15 year lives, and 10% is a common lease rate. The present value of $1, over 15 years, discounted at 10% is 7.61, or around 7.5, which is a typical shortcut factor. We can show this by using the pv formula in Microsoft Excel by letting the pmt (for the annuity) be a single dollar, as illustrated below:

=pv(rate,nper,pmt,fv,type)

=pv(10%,15,-1)

=7.61

From Lowe's note disclosure, the average lease payment over the next 5 years is about 385.8. (That is, 385.8 is the average of 389, 389, 388, 384, 379). The present value of an annuity of $385.8, using the shortcut method of multiplying by 7.5, is $2,894 (7.5*385.8), or rounded, about $3 billion. Thus, we would want to add about $3 billion to Lowe's Balance Sheet. The analytical journal entry would be as follows.

Assets		Liabilities		Owners' Equity	
+ 3 billion	Leased Assets	+ 3 billion	Lease Liabilities		

Why would we want to do this when it is not allowed under current U.S. and IASB GAAP? This is a good question. The rules are controversial and are being debated again. It is quite possible that these "off-balance-sheet" amounts will one day be brought "on-balance-sheet" by a new accounting standard. In the meantime, since these leases are non-cancelable and are similar to debt, including them with other debt items will give a more realistic economic picture, irrespective of the executory nature of the contracts. When we calculate ratios, we will include the effects of operating leases.

Now let's turn to the Cash Flow Statement:

Lowe's Cash Flow Statement

For the years ended on	January 30, 2009	February 1, 2008	February 2, 2007
Cash flows from operating activities:			
Net earnings	2,195	2,809	3,105
Adjustments to reconcile net earnings to net cash provided by operating activities:			
Depreciation and amortization	1,667	1,464	1,237
Deferred income taxes	69	2	(6)
Loss on property and other Assets	89	51	23
Loss on redemption of long-term debt	8	-	-
Transaction loss from exchange rate changes	3	-	-
Share-based payment expense	95	99	62
Changes in operating Assets and Liabilities:			
Merchandise inventory – net	(611)	(464)	(509)
Other operating assets	31	(64)	(135)
Accounts payable	402	185	692
Other operating liabilities	174	265	33
Net cash provided by operating activities	**4,122**	**4,347**	**4,502**
Cash flows from investing activities:			
Purchases of short-term investments	(210)	(920)	(284)
Proceeds from sale/maturity of short-term investments	431	1,183	572
Purchases of long-term investments	(1,148)	(1,588)	(558)

Proceeds from sale/maturity of long-term investments	994	1,162	415
Increase in other long-term assets	(56)	(7)	(16)
Property acquired	(3,266)	(4,010)	(3,916)
Proceeds from sale of property and other long-term assets	29	57	72
Net cash used in investing activities	**(3,226)**	**(4,123)**	**(3,715)**
Cash flows from financing activities:			
Net (decrease) increase in short-term borrowings	(57)	1,041	23
Proceeds from issuance of long-term debt	15	1,296	989
Repayment of long-term debt	(573)	(96)	(33)
Proceeds from issuance of common stock under employee stock purchase plan	76	80	76
Proceeds from issuance of common stock from stock options exercised	98	69	100
Cash dividend payments	(491)	(428)	(276)
Repurchase of common stock	(8)	(2,275)	(1,737)
Excess tax benefits of share-based payments	1	6	12
Net cash used in financing activities	**(939)**	**(307)**	**(846)**
Effect of exchange rate changes on cash	**7**	**-**	**-**
Net decrease in cash and cash equivalents	(36)	(83)	(59)
Cash and cash equivalents, beginning of year	281	364	423
Cash and cash equivalents, end of year	**245**	**281**	**364**

Lowe's generated significant cash from operations ($4,122 million), but this is the lowest amount reported over the 3 years, indicating the trend is downward.

As an example of cash flows from investing activities, Lowe's spent $3,266 million on "property acquired," which will include property, buildings, and equipment. Generally, we call property acquired "capital expenditures," or "capex" for short. This is a significant reduction from the previous year's capex ($4,010).

As part of cash flows from financing activities, Lowe's paid down long-term debt by $573 million. Other financing activities include paying dividends to the owners. Lowe's paid dividends totaling $491 million. Another payment to owners would be repurchases of stock. These cash payments to investors, like dividends, are classified as cash for financing activities. Whereas in the previous two years (2006 and 2007), Lowe's bought back $1,737 million and $2,275 million worth of stock from stockholders, respectively, it ceased major share repurchases in 2008.

Now that we have toured the Financial Statements, let's turn to Lowe's Item 7 (Management Discussion and Analysis (MD&A)), to see what management has to say about the financial condition of the firm. To find the MD&A, we go to the beginning of Seq 6, the same subdocument of the 10-K that contains the Financial Statements.

Item 7 of the 10-K: Management Discussion and Analysis

Above we spotted a few short term trends and major changes in some of the account balances, such as Long Term Debt. Additionally, some of the common size ratios changed significantly, such as the common size SG&A Expense Ratio. Firms are required to discuss their Financial Statements. The SEC requires this discussion in Item 7. By requiring the MD&A, the SEC is suggesting that the numbers from the accounting process are insufficient for lenders and investors to come to an understanding of the firm.

Included in the MD&A are reasons for changes in "line items" in the Financial Statements. For instance, we know that revenues fell slightly, but we would like management to discuss the reasons for the change and perhaps what they plan to do about it going forward. Firms must also discuss any known trends and uncertainties, both favorable and unfavorable, which may impact future operations. They must also provide disclosures about "off-balance-sheet obligations." These are obligations that are not recognized as liabilities in the Balance Sheet, simply because the accounting standards do not (yet) require Financial Statement recognition.

Firms must also discuss future capital expenditures, liquidity needs, and sources of liquidity. All of these types of disclosures are expected to augment the numbers in the Financial Statements so that lenders and investors can have a better picture of how the firm is doing and where the firm may be heading.

Below we provide excerpts from Lowe's MD&A (from the 10-K), followed by a discussion of some of the highlights:

External Factors Impacting Our Business

We entered 2008 knowing a challenging sales environment would pressure our results, but the effects of declining home prices, rising unemployment and tightening credit markets were even greater than anticipated. Highlighting the impact of the current economic environment on our business, comparable store sales declined 7.2% in 2008, while gross margin declined 43 basis points versus the prior year. The economic pressures on consumers intensified in the fourth quarter as unemployment swelled, resulting in a further decline in consumer confidence and consumer spending. In fact, consumer spending continued to contract at the fastest rate in over 25 years. For the fourth quarter of 2008, comparable store sales declined 9.9%, while gross margin declined 115 basis points versus the fourth quarter of 2007.

During the fourth quarter 2008 holiday season, as consumer spending contracted substantially, we knew that competition for sales would be intense in certain categories where we compete with a broader group of retailers. During one of the most promotional holiday seasons in memory, we chose to be proactive and move more quickly and deeply than originally planned with our seasonal merchandise markdowns. We also accelerated our exit strategy for the majority of our wallpaper product group. These more aggressive merchandise markdowns pressured gross margin in the fourth quarter of 2008, but improved our inventory position heading into 2009. We expect our first quarter 2009 gross margin to recover and be down only slightly compared to the first quarter of 2008.

For the year, we estimate that the discretionary component of our sales declined to approximately one-third of total sales, down from approximately 45% in 2006, as the number and size of discretionary projects continued to decline. This hesitancy to invest in larger discretionary projects led to a decline of 9% in comparable store sales for tickets above $500 during the year. However, tickets below $50 experienced only a 2% decline in comparable store sales in 2008, evidence of the relative strength of smaller-ticket items.

The sales environment remains challenging, and the external pressures facing our industry will continue in 2009. The potential for a recovery in demand during 2009 is primarily dependent on factors beyond our control, with stabilizing employment statistics being one of the most important in restoring consumer spending. With the uncertainty in the current environment, we remain focused on effectively deploying capital, controlling expenses and capturing profitable market share.

Effectively Deploying Capital

We have looked critically at our capital plan for 2009 and have reduced our planned store openings to 60 to 70 stores, inclusive of approximately five store openings in Canada and two store openings in Mexico. This is down from 115 store openings in 2008. The reduction in store openings is in response to the challenging economic environment in markets across the U.S. We are also rationalizing other capital spending, including our store remerchandising efforts, to ensure an appropriate return on our investment. These changes have reduced our capital plan to $2.5 billion in 2009, a reduction of $1.1 billion compared to our capital spending in 2008.

Controlling Expenses

Our largest expense is payroll, and we strive to keep payroll hours in our stores proportionate to sales volumes and, even more specifically, to the sales volumes of individual departments within our stores. Our goal is to manage our payroll expense without sacrificing customer service, which is accomplished with the staffing model we have built over many years. The staffing model is reviewed regularly to incorporate improvements and efficiencies we have implemented that have allowed us to move non-selling hours to selling hours. Examples of such improvements in 2008 include our Freight Flow initiative that took best practices from our receiving process and implemented them across the chain. In addition, during 2008, we reduced store hours in some of our slower sales markets when Daylight Saving Time ended, which allowed us to reallocate hours in affected stores to the busier times of the day. As a result of these improvements, we have updated our staffing model for 2009, reducing the required hours and reducing the base hours threshold without reducing customer facing hours. We will continue to monitor our service levels closely throughout 2009 to ensure these changes to our staffing model do not negatively impact customer service.

We have also reviewed our physical inventory process to identify process improvements and cost savings. The majority of our stores has historically had two physical inventories per year; however, during the past several years our inventory shrink control initiatives have yielded solid results. As a result, we began a test of conducting one physical inventory in our better-performing stores. Over the past four years, we have slowly increased the number of stores with one physical inventory and have experienced no noticeable increases in those stores' shrink results. Therefore, we are moving additional stores to one inventory per year in 2009, which will save approximately $10 million.

Fiscal 2008 Compared to Fiscal 2007

Net sales – Reflective of the challenging sales environment, net sales decreased 0.1% to $48.2 billion in 2008. Comparable store sales declined 7.2% in 2008 compared to a decline of 5.1% in 2007. Total customer transactions increased 2.8% compared to 2007, driven by our store expansion program. However, average ticket decreased 2.8% to $65.15, as a result of fewer project sales. Comparable store customer transactions declined 4.1%, and comparable store average ticket declined 3.1% compared to 2007.

The sales weakness we continued to experience was most pronounced in larger discretionary projects and was the result of dramatic reductions in consumer spending. Certain of our project categories, including cabinets & countertops and millwork, had double-digit declines in comparable store sales for the year. These two project categories together with flooring were approximately 17% of our total sales in 2008. This is comparable to 2002 levels, after having peaked at nearly 18.5% in 2006. We also experienced continued weakness in certain of our style categories, such as fashion plumbing, lighting and windows & walls. These product categories are also typically more discretionary in nature and delivered double-digit declines in comparable store sales for the year.

Gross margin – For 2008, gross margin of 34.21% represented a 43-basis-point decrease from 2007. This decrease was primarily driven by carpet installation and other promotions, which negatively impacted gross margin by approximately 21 basis points. We also saw a decline of approximately 14 basis points due to higher fuel prices during the first half of the year and de-leverage in distribution fixed costs. Additionally, markdowns associated with our decision to exit wallpaper reduced gross margin by approximately three basis points. The de-leverage from these factors was partially offset by a positive impact of approximately 12 basis points from lower inventory shrink and approximately four basis points attributable to the mix of products sold.

Cash flows from operating activities continue to provide the primary source of our liquidity. The change in cash flows from operating activities in 2008 compared to 2007 resulted primarily from decreased net earnings and an increase in inventory. This change was partially offset by an increase in accounts payable, which is a result of our continued efforts to improve vendor payment terms. The change in cash flows from operating activities in 2007 compared to 2006 resulted primarily from decreased net earnings and an increase in inventory as a result of our store expansion program, partially offset by an increase in deferred revenue associated with our extended warranty program.

Sources of Liquidity

In addition to our cash flows from operations, additional liquidity is provided by our short-term borrowing facilities. We have a $1.75 billion senior credit facility that expires in June 2012. The senior credit facility supports our commercial paper and revolving credit programs. The senior credit facility has a $500 million letter of credit sublimit. Amounts outstanding under letters of credit reduce the amount available for borrowing under the senior credit facility. Borrowings made are unsecured and are priced at fixed rates based upon market conditions at the time of funding in accordance with the terms of the senior credit facility. The senior credit facility contains certain restrictive covenants, which include maintenance of a debt leverage ratio, as defined by the senior credit facility. We were in compliance with those covenants at January 30, 2009. Nineteen banking institutions are participating in the senior credit facility. As of January 30, 2009, there was $789 million outstanding under the commercial paper program, all of which was issued in the fourth quarter.

Our debt ratings at January 30, 2009, were as follows:

Current Debt Ratings	S&P	Moody's	Fitch
Commercial Paper	A1	P1	F1
Senior Debt	A+	A1	A+
Outlook	**Stable**	**Stable**	**Negative**

Cash Requirements
Capital expenditures

Our 2009 capital budget is approximately $2.5 billion, inclusive of approximately $300 million of lease commitments, resulting in a net cash outflow of $2.2 billion in 2009. Approximately 72% of this planned commitment is for store expansion. Our expansion plans for 2009 consist of 60 to 70 new stores and are expected to increase sales floor square footage by approximately 4%. Approximately 98% of the 2009 projects will be owned, which includes approximately 35% ground-leased properties.

Our share repurchase program is implemented through purchases made from time to time either in the open market or through private transactions. Shares purchased under the share repurchase program are retired and returned to authorized and unissued status. During 2008, there were no share repurchases under the share repurchase program. As of January 30, 2009, we had remaining authorization through fiscal 2009 under the share repurchase program of $2.2 billion.

We believe that net cash provided by operating and financing activities will be adequate for our expansion plans and for our other operating requirements over the next 12 months. The availability of funds through the issuance of commercial paper or new debt or the borrowing cost of these funds could be adversely affected due to a debt rating downgrade, which we do not expect, or a deterioration of certain financial ratios. In addition, continuing volatility in the global capital markets may affect our ability to access those markets for additional borrowings or increase costs associated with those borrowings. There are no provisions in any agreements that would require early cash settlement of existing debt or leases as a result of a downgrade in our debt rating or a decrease in our stock price.

LOWE'S BUSINESS OUTLOOK

As of February 20, 2009, the date of our fourth quarter 2008 earnings release, we expected to open 60 to 70 stores during 2009, resulting in total square footage growth of approximately 4%. We expected total sales in 2009 to range from a decline of

2% to an increase of 2% and comparable store sales to decline 4% to 8%. Earnings before interest and taxes as a percentage of sales (operating margin) was expected to decline approximately 170 basis points. In addition, store opening costs were expected to be approximately $50 million. Diluted earnings per share of $1.04 to $1.20 were expected for the fiscal year ending January 29, 2010. Our outlook for 2009 does not assume any share repurchases.

The following table summarizes our significant contractual obligations and commercial commitments:

Contractual Obligations (In millions)	Total	Less than 1 year	3 years	4 – 5 years	After 5 years
Long-term debt (principal and interest amounts, excluding discount)	9,256	294	1,044	1,025	6,893
Capital lease obligations[1]	543	63	122	121	237
Operating leases[1]	6,185	389	777	763	4,256
Purchase obligations[2]	995	620	345	16	14
Total contractual obligations	16,979	1,366	2,288	1,925	11,400

Let's recap what we learned in the above excerpts.

The economic environment was difficult all year, but particularly in the fourth quarter. Gross margins were pressured because of aggressive markdowns on inventory. Sales weakness was pronounced in big ticket, "discretionary" items. The outlook for 2009 is not rosy. Lowe's will control expenses (primarily payroll, which is part of SG&A Expense), "effectively deploy capital" (by further cutting capital expenditures to $2.5 billion), and try to capture market share from other retailers as a way of growing. The firm still has adequate cash flow (liquidity), both from its own Cash Flows from Operations, as well as access to bank loans, although Fitch (a "credit rating" agency) has a negative outlook on the firm's debt.

Lowe's also gives official guidance in its MD&A (see "Lowe's Business Outlook"). It is rare for a firm to do this. Most firms that give guidance do so in conference calls and press releases, rather than incorporating it into the MD&A. The guidance is mainly in the form of predicted ranges. For instance, Diluted EPS is expected to be in the range of $1.04 to 1.20. What if Lowe's misses the target and next year's EPS is only $1.00? As long as Lowe's has a sound basis for its prediction and makes it in "good faith," the firm is protected from legal action under U.S. securities laws.

The final item in the excerpt from the MD&A is a table that shows all contractual obligations of the firm. Some of these items are found in the Financial Statements and recognized as liabilities, but not all of them are. For instance, under existing accounting rules in the U.S., as we mentioned earlier, "operating leases" are not shown as a liability.

There is much more in the 10-K. However, we have hit many of the highlights. We have a fairly good picture of Lowe's current situation and an idea about what its 12-month future could look like.

OTHER SOURCES OF INFORMATION

CEO Letter to Shareholders

Not all firms' CEOs write letters to their shareholders, but most do. The letter may not contain specific guidance, but often the CEO will give a "big picture" view of the firm's opportunities and risks, and he or she may also provide some information on strategy that would also help build the financial model.

To obtain the CEO's letter, we must usually go to the firm's website and download the firm's "annual report." The annual report contains the Financial Statements, the notes, and the MD&A (just like the 10-K), but it also contains pictures and graphs, which are often interesting to view to get a better idea of what the company does and where they operate. Although the 10-K is a more complete source of information, it curiously does not contain the CEO's letter.

To obtain the annual report, we go to LOW's website (www.lowes.com), and we look for "About Lowe's," and then for "Investors," and then for "Lowe's Annual Reports." Here, we can obtain and download a pdf file for the most recent annual report.

Below are certain relevant excerpts from the letter from the CEO (from the 2008 annual report):

> As we think about 2009, we know the economic backdrop will be as bad, if not worse, than in 2008. Comparable store sales will likely be negative for a third consecutive year. As we plan for another difficult sales environment, we remain focused on opportunities to reduce expenses.
>
> We know one sure way to lose market share is to reduce expenses too aggressively and negatively impact customer service.
>
> The key to success in difficult economic times is a focus on what you can control. That is our pledge. Regardless of the expansion or contraction of the industry, we will continue to work diligently to drive sales and capture profitable market share. With a responsibility to tightly manage expenses, we will constantly strive to improve our systems and processes to become more efficient, but we will always balance expense management with our commitment to customer service. These efforts will ensure we maximize near-term opportunities and position Lowe's for a prosperous future when conditions improve.

We see from above that the CEO acknowledges the issue about expenses, particularly SG&A Expense. We recall from our overview of the Income Statement that SG&A Expense grew YOY 5.3%, whereas sales fell slightly. However, to cut SG&A Expense many mean cutting sales associates, and the CEO alludes to the importance of customer service as part of Lowe's brand. This presents a dilemma for management. It also appears that potential sales increases will come from gains in market share from a stagnant market, if not a declining one. Price pressures will undoubtedly continue in such an environment, given the competitive nature of the industry.

Conference Calls, News Articles, Form 8-K, Insider Transactions, Audit Opinion, Research Reports

While we are at the firm's website, we recommend listening to the firm's most recent "conference call" with analysts. Most firms store archived versions of these conference calls on their websites for several months. The give-and-take between the firm's management and analysts can be quite revealing, and managers often give further guidance on the conference call.

For example (as of this writing), the following site is the location of Lowe's archived conference call. The link to the site is on Lowe's website (at "About Lowe's", then "Investors").

http://investor.shareholder.com/lowes/

Earnings Release Dates	Webcast Events (view archive)
1Q10 Mon., May 17, 2010	**Morgan Stanley Retail Field Trip**
2Q10 Mon., Aug 16, 2010	03/16/10 at 8:45 AM
3Q10 Mon., Nov 15, 2010	**CT Lowe's Fourth Quarter and Fiscal Year 2009**
4Q10 Wed., Feb 23, 2011	**Earnings Conference Call**
	02/22/10 at 9:00 AM ET
	2009 Analyst & Investor Conference Webcast
	09/22/09 at 10:00 AM ET

As we see, the webcasts that are listed include one for the "Fourth Quarter and Fiscal Year 2009 Earnings Conference Call." (We also note that Lowe's lists it Earnings Release Dates. Not all firms do this, but many of the larger ones do.)

When U.S. firms release their earnings, they furnish the release to the SEC on Form 8-K. The 8-K filing precedes the 10-Q for quarterly earnings releases and the 10-K for annual earnings releases. The 8-K is called the "Current Report" and is issued for major, current events, such as earnings releases, but also events such as changes in top management. The purpose of the 8-K is to bring more timely information to the markets, so that market participants do not have to wait for quarterly or annual filings. Therefore, we also recommend checking the SEC's website for recent 8-Ks.

For those 8-Ks that provide earnings releases, often firms will provide details about the Earnings Conference Call. For instance, the 8-K below shows how we could actually participate in Lowe's conference call. (Rather than typing in "10-K," as we did before, we simply type in "8-K" to obtain these filings.)

UNITED STATES
SECURITIES AND EXCHANGE COMMISSION
Washington, D.C. 20549

FORM 8-K

CURRENT REPORT
Pursuant To Section 13 or 15 (d) of the Securities Exchange Act of 1934
Date of Report (Date of earliest event reported) February 22, 2010

A conference call to discuss fourth quarter 2009 operating results is scheduled for today (Monday, February 22) at 9:00 am EST. Please dial 888-817-4020 (international callers dial 706-679-4821) to participate. A webcast of the call will take place simultaneously and can be accessed by visiting Lowe's website at www.Lowes.com/investor and clicking on Lowe's Fourth Quarter and Fiscal Year 2009 Earnings Conference Call Webcast. A replay of the call will be archived on Lowes.com until May 16, 2010.

We also recommend searching for recent news articles and press releases. Simple web searches can turn up recent information that may be timelier than SEC filings. Bing, Google, Yahoo, and Lexis-Nexis searches are quick and easy and well worth the effort.

It is also worth looking to see if there are major "insider transactions." Insider transactions are transactions where managers buy or sell the firm's stock. If managers are suddenly selling "a lot" of shares, it raises questions. Although data on insider transactions are available through another form at the SEC website, it is usually easier to check other websites. If we do not have access to subscription based services (such as Bloomberg, CapIQ, Factset, etc.), we could even check with free sites, such as finance.google.com or finance.yahoo.com. At websites such as these, after typing in the firm's name or ticker symbol, we will be able to find links to "major holders" and "insider transactions." We may need context to know whether these insider transactions (of which there are many) are significant. Thus, we may need to search for news reports to see if there are stories circulating about "significant" changes in insider ownership.

We also need to check the audit opinion. Almost all are "clean" opinions, but it's worth a look, regardless. To find the letter from the auditor, we go to the 10-K. A search for the phrase "present fairly" will usually direct us to the most important part of the audit letter. This is the phrase that we look for to make sure that the audit opinion section of the audit letter is clean. We have put the audit opinion for Lowe's in bold font below:

REPORT OF INDEPENDENT REGISTERED PUBLIC ACCOUNTING FIRM

To the Board of Directors and Shareholders of Lowe's Companies, Inc.
Mooresville, North Carolina

We have audited the accompanying consolidated balance sheets of Lowe's Companies, Inc. and subsidiaries (the "Company") as of January 30, 2009 and February 1, 2008, and the related consolidated statements of earnings, shareholders' equity, and cash flows for each of the three fiscal years in the period ended January 30, 2009. These Financial Statements are the responsibility of the Company's management. Our responsibility is to express an opinion on these Financial Statements based on our audits.

We conducted our audits in accordance with the standards of the Public Company Accounting Oversight Board (United States). Those standards require that we plan and perform the audit to obtain reasonable assurance about whether the Financial Statements are free of material misstatement. An audit includes examining, on a test basis, evidence supporting the amounts and disclosures in the Financial Statements. An audit also includes assessing the accounting principles used and significant estimates made by management, as well as evaluating the overall financial statement presentation. We believe that our audits provide a reasonable basis for our opinion.

In our opinion, such consolidated Financial Statements present fairly, in all material respects, the financial position of the Company at January 30, 2009 and February 1, 2008, and the results of its operations and its cash flows for each of the three fiscal years in the period ended January 30, 2009, in conformity with accounting principles generally accepted in the United States of America.

We have also audited, in accordance with the standards of the Public Company Accounting Oversight Board (United States), the Company's internal control over financial reporting as of January 30, 2009, based on the criteria established in Internal Control-Integrated Framework issued by the Committee of Sponsoring Organizations of the Treadway Commission and our report dated March 31, 2009 expressed an unqualified opinion on the Company's internal control over financial reporting.

/s/Deloitte & Touche LLP
March 31, 2009

> **HINT**
>
> When searching for specific words or phrases in an electronic document use "Control F" (or "Ctrl F"). Most
> software utilizes these common key strokes, thus making your analysis more efficient!

We also recommend seeing what research analysts are saying about a firm. Some research reports are free at the various research institutions (such as banks), but most require payment. However, banks will provide their clients with in-house research reports. It is also worth noting that universities often subscribe to several research databases that include analyst reports.

Research analysts have a deep understanding of the firms they cover and such understanding can be extremely insightful. If access to research reports is problematic, we can find a summary of what analysts think about a particular firm, particularly as it relates to buying or selling the firm's shares of stock. For instance, if we go to finance.yahoo.com, type in the firm's ticker symbol and look for "Analyst Opinion," we can see what the average opinion is.

PUTTING IT THE ANALYSIS TOGETHER – QUALITATIVE AND QUANTITATIVE ASSESSMENTS

We will put together our picture of LOW thus far in the below matrix. Much of the below analysis is subjective and based upon inferences from reading the above excerpts.

What are the major trends in industry?	Housing starts, existing home sales, employment rate, and household income continue to be under pressure.
What are the firm's strengths?	Lowe's has developed a brand with characteristics of consumer friendliness, customer support, store layout and design (and cleanliness). They also have a wide selection of products at "everyday low prices." They have considerable purchasing power.
What are the firm's weaknesses?	Lowe's is not as penetrated in certain markets as is the chief competitor (The Home Depot).
What are the firm's opportunities?	Lowe's has expansion opportunities in urban markets and overseas. Lowe's goal is to gain market share in these tough economic times.
What are the firm's threats?	Competition from other "big box" retailers, the rough economy and related housing issues represent threats to their future. The CEO is not positive about 2009.
What is the firm's strategy?	Lowe's is growing organically into urban markets and continuing to develop a distinctive brand.
How is the firm implementing the strategy?	Lowe's is still implementing urban market penetration in spite of the economy and is not laying off employees in order to maintain service levels (as part of its brand development). However, it will focus on cost control and strategic capital expenditures.
What are other "key performance indicators"?	Lowe's cites average ticket, sales per square foot, and transactions per year. All of these declined considerably over the last year.
Does the firm have pressing liquidity needs (short and long term)?	This does not currently appear to be problematic according to the MD&A. Lowe's continues to generate operating cash flow and has access to credit.

Does the firm have major Contingencies or Litigation?	This does not currently appear to be problematic according to Item 3 in the 10-K.
What is the average analyst rating?	Out of 22 analysts, the average rating is 2.2, on a 5 point scale, where 1 is "strong buy" and 5 is "sell," as per finance.yahoo.com.
Was the audit opinion a clean opinion?	Yes.
What is major current news?	No major news as of this writing.
What is firm's credit rating (S&P)?	A+, according to S&P, as provided in the MD&A.
What is the Cash Flow Profile (multiyear)?	See below.
What is the stock price performance?	See below.

The Cash Flow Profile plots Cash Flows from Operations (CFO), Cash Flows from Investing Activities (CFI), and Cash Flows from Financing Activities (CFF), as well as Net Income, over multiple years in order to try to spot where LOW might be in its life cycle:

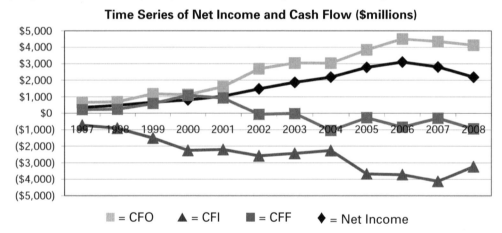

Time Series of Net Income and Cash Flow ($millions)

■ = CFO   ▲ = CFI   ■ = CFF   ♦ = Net Income

As we see in the graph, both Net Income and CFO have grown dramatically (positively) over the years. CFI has grown too, but it slopes downward to indicate that more and more cash is going out of Lowe's as the firm invests in buildings and real estate. CFF goes up and stays positive until about 2001/2002. This means that Lowe's had cash coming in from borrowings and other sources for various financing needs. In 2004, Lowe's financing cash flows turned negative, meaning that it returned cash to lenders and stockholders in the form of debt reduction, dividends, and share repurchases.

What is rather unusual is that Lowe's was able to grow and simultaneously return large amounts of cash to investors during the growth phase. This indicates financial strength and flexibility, at least over this period of time. Generally, it appears that Lowe's is still in the growth phase, but growth is slowing. CFO has dipped, as has Net Income. Although CFI is negative, meaning that Lowe's has continued to invest in capital expenditures (capex), it is slowing considerably, reflecting the general economic conditions, particularly in the housing market.

In general, CFO, NI, and CFI have all been decelerating over the last couple of years. Lowe's appears to maintain considerable financial flexibility, allowing it to continue to invest in new stores (albeit at a slower rate) without net outside financing.

Lowe's stock price history is below:

Price Per Common Share

The downturn in the housing market has not been kind to Lowe's stock price, as indicated above. Lowe's stock price is below where it was 5 years earlier, according to the graph. It appeared to peak toward the end of 2005 and 2006.

We now turn to creating some relevant ratios for Lowe's as we move to the more quantitative analysis.

However, let's be reminded of a few of the ratio warnings that we listed in the FFAA Handbook:

- We need to be aware of what we are trying to measure with a ratio. Most ratios are proxies for an underlying construct, which we cannot measure scientifically.

- We need to choose only those ratios that are relevant for our particular firm.

- Ratios can badly mis-measure a construct, so we need to think about why we obtain a particular result if it is unusual. For instance, we would want to investigate further if we were to obtain high profitability measures for a firm that is known to be in severe distress.

- Ratios need to be benchmarked in order to interpret them in any meaningful way.

- Ratios built on historical financial results are not necessarily (if at all) good predictors of the future.

- Ratios are not standardized. It is important to be consistent in calculating ratios, and, if obtained from a third party, it is important to know how the ratios are calculated.

We now turn to Lowe's Income Statement. Note that we input Lowe's financial data into a spreadsheet for analytical purposes. (This is sometimes called "doing the spreads" on a firm.) The spreadsheet allows us more efficiently to compare firms with varying account titles and statement formats. For instance, on the Balance Sheet, we combine all Owners' Equity accounts into one line, called "Equity". We rarely need the details of Owners' Equity for calculating ratios or for financial modeling, and Owners' Equity can vary substantially from firm to firm both in the number of accounts and account titles.

In the below template for the Income Statement, we will first consider YOY and CS ratios.

LOW	2008	2007	2006	YOY	YOY	CS	CS	CS
Revenues	48,230	48,283	46,927	(0.1%)	2.9%	100.0%	100.0%	100.0%
Cost of Sales	(31,729)	(31,556)	(30,729)	0.5%	2.7%	65.8%	65.4%	65.5%
SG&A Expense	(11,074)	(10,515)	(9,738)	5.3%	8.0%	23.0%	21.8%	20.8%
Depreciation Expense	(1,539)	(1,366)	(1,162)	12.7%	17.6%	3.2%	2.8%	2.5%
Net Interest Expense	(280)	(194)	(154)	44.3%	26.0%	0.6%	0.4%	0.3%
Store Opening Costs	(102)	(141)	(146)	(27.7%)	(3.4%)	0.2%	0.3%	0.3%
Income Before Income Taxes	3,506	4,511	4,998	(22.3%)	(9.7%)	7.3%	9.3%	10.7%
Provision for Income Taxes	(1,311)	(1,702)	(1,893)	(23.0%)	(10.1%)	2.7%	3.5%	4.0%
Net Income	**2,195**	**2,809**	**3,105**	**(21.9%)**	**(9.5%)**	**4.6%**	**5.8%**	**6.6%**
Basic EPS	1.51	1.90						
Fully Diluted EPS	1.49	1.86						
Dividends per Share	0.335	0.29						

We note that Revenues fell by 0.1% YOY, compared to a 2.9% increase for the previous fiscal year. Additionally, Cost of Sales (COGS) grew at .5% and SG&A grew at 5.3%. The combination of falling revenues with rising COGS and SG&A Expense hurt margins and Net Income. Also, a surge in YOY Net Interest Expense (44.3%) and Depreciation Expense (12.7%) contributed to the fall in the bottom line (Net Income) of 21.9%.

Below are Lowe's Balance Sheets and related YOY and Common Size ratios:

LOW	2008	2007	2006	YOY	YOY	CS	CS
Cash and Cash Equivalents	245	281	364	(12.8%)	(22.8%)	0.7%	0.9%
Short-term Investments	416	249	432	67.1%	(42.4%)	1.3%	0.8%
Accounts and Notes Receivable, net	0	0	0	n/a	n/a	0.0%	0.0%
Inventories	8,209	7,611	7,144	7.9%	6.5%	25.1%	24.7%
Other Current Assets	381	545	374	(30.1%)	45.7%	1.2%	1.8%
Total Current Assets	9,251	8,686	8,314	6.5%	4.5%	28.3%	28.1%
Property, Plant and Equipment, net	22,722	21,361	18,971	6.4%	12.6%	69.5%	69.2%
Investments	253	509	165	(50.3%)	208.5%	0.8%	1.6%
Other Non Current Assets	460	313	317	47.0%	(1.3%)	1.4%	1.0%
Total Assets	**32,686**	**30,869**	**27,767**	**5.9%**	**11.2%**	**100.0%**	**100.0%**
Accounts Payable	4,109	3,713	3,524	10.7%	5.4%	12.6%	12.0%
Current Maturities of Long Term Debt	1,021	1,104	88	(7.5%)	1,154.5%	3.1%	3.6%
Other Current Liabilities	2,892	2,934	2,927	(1.4%)	0.2%	8.8%	9.5%
Total Current Liabilities	8,022	7,751	6,539	3.5%	18.5%	24.5%	25.1%
Long-Term Debt Obligations	5,039	5,576	4,325	(9.6%)	28.9%	15.4%	18.1%
Deferred Income Taxes	660	670	735	(1.5%)	(8.8%)	2.0%	2.2%
Other Non Current Liabilities	910	774	443	17.6%	74.7%	2.8%	2.5%
Equity (combined)	18,055	16,098	15,725	12.2%	2.4%	55.2%	52.1%
Total Liabilities and Owners' Equity	**32,686**	**30,869**	**27,767**	**5.9%**	**11.2%**	**100.0%**	**100.0%**

Inventory comprises about 25.1% of total assets, up from 24.7% in the previous year. Additionally, YOY inventory growth (7.9%) was much more than the YOY Revenue change (-0.1%, as shown on the Income Statement), which is problematic.

Above, we also see that Long Term Debt Obligations declined YOY by 9.6%. Lowe's retired debt during the year, as seen below in the excerpts from the Cash Flow Statement:

LOW	2008	2007	2006	YOY	YOY
Total Cash from Operations (CFO)	**4,122**	**4,347**	**4,502**	**(5.2%)**	**(3.4%)**
Capital Expenditures	(3,266)	(4,010)	(3,916)	(18.6%)	2.4%
Total Cash from Investing Activities (CFI)	**(3,226)**	**(4,123)**	**(3,715)**	**(21.8%)**	**11.0%**
Net Change in Debt	(615)	2,241	979	(127.4%)	128.9%
Dividends	(491)	(428)	(276)	14.7%	55.1%
Share Repurchase	(8)	(2,275)	(1,737)	(99.6%)	31.0%
Total Cash from Financing Activities (CFF)	**(939)**	**(307)**	**(846)**	**205.9%**	**(63.7%)**

Lowe's generated $4,122 million in CFO, down 5.2% YOY. Capital expenditures fell significantly for the most recent YOY (by 18.6%) to $3,266 million. Lowe's increased its dividend by 14.7%, but it virtually ceased share repurchases, which fell to only $8 million.

We now turn to various performance and risk ratios. The ratios in the below table are the same as for our stylized example in Chapter 8 of the FFAA Handbook. For a review of how these ratios are calculated, please refer to that chapter. We provide a few comments below the table.

LOW	Commonly used Ratios and other Measures	2008	2007	2006
1	Profit Margin	4.6%	5.8%	6.6%
2	Asset Turnover	1.5	1.6	1.7
3	Leverage	1.8	1.9	1.8
4	Return on Equity (ROE)	12.2%	17.4%	19.7%
5	Return on Assets (ROA)	6.7%	9.1%	11.2%
6	Earnings Before Interest and Taxes (EBIT)	3,888.0	4,846.0	5,298.0
7	Earnings Before Interest, Taxes, Dep. and Amort. (EBITDA)	5,555.0	6,310.0	6,535.0
8	Effective Tax Rate	37.4%	37.7%	37.9%
9	After Tax EBIT or NOPAT (Net operating profit after tax)	2434.2	3,017.6	3,291.4
10	Market Capitalization (Market Cap)	22,593.9	34,379.6	48,281.5
11	ROIC (using market value for equity)	8.5%		
12	Total Returns to Shareholders (TRS)	(33.4%)		
13	Cost Ratio	65.8%	65.4%	65.5%
14	Gross Margin	34.2%	34.6%	34.5%
15	SG&A Ratio	23.0%	21.8%	20.8%
16	R&D Ratio	0.0%	0.0%	0.0%
17	EBIT Margin (Operating Margin)	8.1%	10.0%	11.3%

18	Accounts Receivable Turnover	n/a	n/a	n/a
19	Inventory Turnover	3.9	4.1	4.3
20	Days Sales Outstanding (DSO)	n/a	n/a	n/a
21	Days Sales in Inventory (DSI)	94.4	88.0	84.9
22	Operating Cycle	n/a	n/a	n/a
23	Purchases	32,327.0	32,023.0	
24	Accounts Payable Turnover	7.9	8.6	
25	Days Payable Outstanding (DPO)	46.4	42.3	
26	Cash Cycle (days other financing required)	n/a	n/a	n/a
27	Current Ratio	1.2	1.1	1.3
28	Quick Ratio	0.1	0.1	0.1
29	Total Debt to Total Capital	25.1%	29.3%	21.9%
30	Interest Coverage	13.9	25.0	34.4
31	Cash Interest Coverage	18.0	31.7	37.5
32	Effective Interest Rate (pre tax)	4.6%	2.9%	3.5%
33	Effective Interest Rate (after tax)	2.9%	1.8%	2.2%
34	Dividend Payout Ratio	22.4%	15.2%	8.9%
35	Dividend Yield	2.2%	1.2%	0.6%

The numerical references below **(in bold parentheses)** refer to the numbered list above.

LOW's profit margin declined dramatically from 2007 to 2008 **(1)**. Asset turns **(2)** also declined, as did leverage **(3)**. Therefore, ROE fell significantly (from 17.4% to 12.2%) **(4)**, as did ROA **(5)**. Shareholders were probably "not happy" with their total returns **(12)**. The cost ratio **(13)** and gross margin ratio **(14)** also deteriorated. Common size SG&A **(15)**, worsened as it rose from 21.8% to 23.0%. Inventory turns **(19)** and DSI **(21)** deteriorated considerably. It takes LOW 94.4 days on average to sell its inventory, up from 88 days. LOW was slower in paying its suppliers by about 4 days **(25)**, from 42.3 days to 46.4 days.

All ratios related to Accounts Receivable are not available, because LOW sells all its Accounts Receivable. Ratios that are related to Accounts Receivable include **(18)**, **(20)**, **(22)**, and **(26)**. Therefore, all of these ratios are shown as "n/a."

Although interest coverage **(30)** and cash interest coverage **(31)** both deteriorated, LOW maintains significant financial flexibility through robust CFO and favorable debt ratings, which LOW reports in its MD&A.

LOW substantially increased its dividend payout **(34)**, in part, however, because of the decline in Net Income. The yield also increased **(35)**, similarly in part because of the falling share price. Nonetheless, the actual dollar-amount of the dividend did increase, as seen in the Statement of Cash Flows (by 14.7%, from $428 million to $491 million).

We need to compare LOW to The Home Depot (ticker symbol: HD) as another point of reference. Since these two firms are similar, it would be insightful to know how LOW's results compared to those of HD. This will give us relative measures about how well the firms were able to manage through difficult times.

Below we provide HD's Income Statement and Balance Sheet, using the identical template (spreadsheet) that we used for LOW:

HD	2008	2007	2006	YOY	YOY	CS	CS	CS
Revenue	71,288	77,349	79,022	(7.8%)	(2.1%)	100.0%	100.0%	100.0%
Cost of Goods Sold	(47,298)	(51,352)	(52,476)	(7.9%)	(2.1%)	66.3%	66.4%	66.4%
SG&A Expense	(17,846)	(17,053)	(16,106)	4.7%	5.9%	25.0%	22.0%	20.4%
Depreciation/ Amortization	(1,785)	(1,702)	(1,574)	4.9%	8.1%	2.5%	2.2%	2.0%
Net Interest Expense	(606)	(622)	(364)	(2.6%)	70.9%	0.9%	0.8%	0.5%
Other	(163)	0	0	n/a	n/a	0.2%	0.0%	0.0%
Income Before Income Taxes	3,590	6,620	8,502	(45.8%)	(22.1%)	5.0%	8.6%	10.8%
Tax Expense	(1,278)	(2,410)	(3,236)	(47.0%)	(25.5%)	1.8%	3.1%	4.1%
Other	(52)	185	495			0.1%	0.2%	0.6%
Net Income	**2,260**	**4,395**	**5,761**	**(48.6%)**	**(23.7%)**	**3.2%**	**5.7%**	**7.3%**
Basic EPS	1.34	2.38						
Fully Diluted EPS	1.34	2.37						
Dividends per Share	0.90	0.90						

HD	2008	2007	YOY	CS	CS
Cash	519	445	16.6%	1.3%	1.0%
Short(term Investments	6	12	(50.0%)	0.0%	0.0%
Accounts Receivable, net	972	1,259	(29.5%)	2.4%	2.8%
Inventories	10,673	11,731	(9.0%)	25.9%	26.5%
Other Current Assets	1,192	1,227	(2.9%)	2.9%	2.8%
Total Current Assets	13,362	14,674	(8.9%)	32.5%	33.1%
Property, Plant and Equipment, net	26,234	27,476	(4.5%)	63.7%	62.0%
Other Non Current Assets	1,568	2,174	(27.9%)	3.8%	4.9%
Total Assets	41,164	44,324	(7.1%)	100.0%	100.0%
Accounts Payable	4,822	5,732	(15.9%)	11.7%	12.9%
Current Maturities of Debt	1,767	300	489.0%	4.3%	0.7%
Other Current Liabilities	4,564	6,674	(31.6%)	11.1%	15.1%
Total Current Liabilities	11,153	12,706	(12.2%)	27.1%	28.7%
Long(Term Debt Obligations	9,667	11,383	(15.1%)	23.5%	25.7%
Deferred Income Taxes	369	688	(46.4%)	0.9%	1.6%
Other Non Current Liabilities	2,198	1,833	19.9%	5.3%	4.1%
Equity (combined)	17,777	17,714	0.4%	43.2%	40.0%
Total Liabilities and Shareholders' Equity	41,164	44,324	(7.1%)	100.0%	100.0%

Below are excerpts from HD's Statement of Cash Flows:

HD	2008	2007	2006	YOY	YOY
Total CFO	**5,528**	**5,727**	**7,661**	**(3.5%)**	**(25.2%)**
Capex	(1,847)	(3,558)	(3,542)	(48.1%)	0.5%
Total CFI	**(1,729)**	**4,758**	**(7,647)**	**(136.3%)**	**(162.2%)**
Net Change in Debt	(2,045)	1,714	8,035	(219.3%)	(78.7%)
Dividends	(1,521)	(1,709)	(1,395)	(11.0%)	22.5%
Share Repurchase	(70)	(10,815)	(6,684)	(99.4%)	61.8%
Total CFF	**(939)**	**(307)**	**(846)**	**205.9%**	**(63.7%)**

Below, we place a few select ratios of LOW and HD side by side. The ratio number corresponds to the ratios defined in Chapter 8 of the FFAA Handbook:

		LOW	HD
HD	**Commonly used Ratios and other Measures**	**2008**	**2008**
1	Profit Margin	4.6%	3.2%
2	Asset Turnover	1.5	1.7
3	Leverage	1.8	2.3
4	Return on Equity (ROE)	12.2%	12.7%
6	Earnings Before Interest and Taxes (EBIT)	3,888.0	4,359.0
8	Effective Tax Rate	37.4%	35.6%
11	ROIC (using market value for equity)	8.5%	5.9%
12	Total Returns to Shareholders (TRS)	(33.4%)	(24.1%)
13	Cost Ratio	65.8%	66.3%
14	Gross Margin	34.2%	33.7%
15	SG&A Ratio	23.0%	25.0%
19	Inventory Turnover	3.9	4.4
21	Days Sales in inventory (DSI)	94.4	82.4
24	Accounts Payable Turnover	7.9	9.6
25	Days Payable Outstanding (DPO)	46.4	38.1
27	Current Ratio	1.2	1.2
29	Total Debt to Total Capital	25.1%	39.1%
30	Interest Coverage	13.9	7.2
31	Cash Interest Coverage	18.0	11.9

The numerical references **(in bold parentheses)** refer to the numbered list above. LOW's profit margin is higher **(1)**, but the asset turnover and leverage are lower, impacting ROE **(4)**. LOW's effective tax rate is significantly higher **(8)**. LOW's asset turnover is worse **(2)** in part because the inventory is not selling as fast. It takes LOW 12 days longer on average to sell its inventory **(21)**.

LOW has better payment terms than HD, as seen in the days to pay suppliers **(25)**. LOW is much less levered than HD **(29)**, which also is corroborated in the coverage ratios **(30, 31)**. In total, LOW controls expenses somewhat better, as seen in the cost ratio and SG&A ratio **(13, 15)**, but is unable to move its inventory as quickly.

We also note that HD spent only $1,847 on capex, compared to $3,266 for LOW, indicating that LOW continues to invest in expansion, even in these difficult times, much more so than HD. However, we also know that LOW plans to curtail future capex even further to $2,500 (from the MD&A).

We need to consider something we pointed out earlier when we considered Lowe's operating leases. We are reminded that these leases are "off-balance-sheet". Regardless, they represent real, non-cancelable obligations of the firm. Moreover, firms with operating leases are using those assets to generate earnings. Thus, we should incorporate the effects of "off-balance-sheet" leases, at least on two of our ratios, ROA and Debt to Capital.

Earlier, we calculated an estimate of the present value of the operating leases. We estimated that Lowe's had about $3 billion (or $3,000 million) of unrecorded Leased Assets and Lease Liabilities.

Below are the calculations of ROA and Debt to Capital, both unadjusted and adjusted to include the additional $3 billion:

		Calculation
ROA	6.7% (Ratio #5)	=2,195 / 32,686
Adjusted ROA	6.2%	=2,195 / (32,686+3,000)
Debt to Capital	25.1% (Ratio #29)	=(1,021+5,039)/(1,021+5,039+18,055)
Adjusted Debt to Capital	33.4%	=(1,021+5,039+3,000)/(1,021+5,039+18,055+3,000)

As we can see, LOW's ROA and Debt to Capital, when adjusted, are quite different from the unadjusted figures. The returns were not as high, and the firm is significantly more levered than it would initially appear. Other measures would be affected by capitalizing operating leases. An example is Interest Coverage, since interest expense would be higher due to the addition of the Lease Liability. Depreciation Expense would also be higher, due to the addition of the Leased Asset, which would be depreciated.

At this point, we have come to the conclusion of our analysis. We hand off to other texts the continuation of the analysis with Steps 4 and 5. Step 4 is Prediction of Relevant Data, such as future cash flows, EPS, or liquidity. Step 5 is Sensitivity Analysis and Final Decision.

To accomplish Step 4, we would use the analysis of historical results and any guidance from management to build a model of Lowe's. Lowe's has in fact given a good deal of helpful information for forecasting a set of Financial Statements. We saw in the MD&A where Lowe's gave us a range of expected EPS, capex, and other items that are central for building a model of Lowe's future. Before making a relevant decision, based upon our purpose for the analysis, we would want to perform an extensive array of sensitivity tests on the major assumptions underlying the model. For instance, we may wish to estimate firm value and that estimate is a function of future cash flows. In turn, cash flows would be affected by gross margins. We may need to test our valuations using a range of possible outcomes for gross margins. Steps 4 and 5 are indeed interesting and worth pursuing, but as we mentioned at the outset, they require significant development to do them justice.

In the next part of this text are numerous exercises that will reinforce the accounting issues introduced in the FFAA Handbook. Internalizing the accounting concepts, terminology, vocabulary, and methodology will increase the ability to understand, and therefore to analyze, the financial condition of a firm. Such increased understanding also helps tremendously in financial modeling and corporate valuation.

Part 2: Practice Exercises to Accompany the FFAA Handbook

The following practice exercises were designed to complement the corresponding chapters in the Fundamentals of Financial Accounting and Analysis (FFAA) Handbook.

Practice Exercises

For use with Handbook Chapter 1

Practice Solutions

For use with Handbook Chapter 1

1A Journalize the below transactions for a firm that is just commencing business:

1. The firm borrows $50 cash. (Use Note Payable.)

Assets		Liabilities		Owners' Equity	

2. The firm sells stock for $20 cash.

Assets		Liabilities		Owners' Equity	

3. The firm buys a building for $30 cash.

Assets		Liabilities		Owners' Equity	

4. The firm buys inventory for $10 cash.

Assets		Liabilities		Owners' Equity	

5. The firm sells $8 of inventory for $30 cash.

Assets		Liabilities		Owners' Equity	

6. Pays wages of $2 cash. (Use Wage Expense.)

Assets		Liabilities		Owners' Equity	

7. Depreciates the Building by $6. (Reduce the Building account and offset this with Depreciation Expense.)

Assets		Liabilities		Owners' Equity	

8. Books $4 of Interest Expense to be paid later. (Use Interest Payable.)

Assets		Liabilities		Owners' Equity	

1A Journalize the below transactions for a firm that is just commencing business:

1. The firm borrows $50 cash. (Use Note Payable.)

Assets		Liabilities		Owners' Equity	
50	Cash	50	Note Pay.		

2. The firm sells stock for $20 cash.

Assets		Liabilities		Owners' Equity	
20	Cash			20	Stock

3. The firm buys a building for $30 cash.

Assets		Liabilities		Owners' Equity	
(30)	Cash				
30	Building				

4. The firm buys inventory for $10 cash.

Assets		Liabilities		Owners' Equity	
(10)	Cash				
10	Inventory				

5. The firm sells $8 of inventory for $30 cash.

Assets		Liabilities		Owners' Equity	
30	Cash			30	Revenue
(8)	Inventory			(8)	COGS

6. Pays wages of $2 cash. (Use Wage Expense.)

Assets		Liabilities		Owners' Equity	
(2)	Cash			(2)	Wage Exp.

7. Depreciates the Building by $6. (Reduce the Building account and offset this with Depreciation Expense.)

Assets		Liabilities		Owners' Equity	
(6)	Building			(6)	Dep. Exp.

8. Books $4 of Interest Expense to be paid later. (Use Interest Payable.)

Assets		Liabilities		Owners' Equity	
		4	Int. Pay.	(4)	Int. Exp.

1A (continued)

9. Books $4 of Tax Expense to be paid later. (Use Tax Payable.)

Assets		Liabilities		Owners' Equity	

1B Post the journal entries to the ledger. The Beginning Balances ("Begin") are all 0 because the firm is just commencing its business. Also note that Event 5 has two parts and is therefore listed twice in the ledger. Post revenue and all expenses directly to Retained Earnings.

	Assets				Liabilities and Owners' Equity					
	Cash	Inventory	Building	Total	Notes Payable	Interest Payable	Taxes Payable	Stock	Retained Earnings	Total
Begin	0	0	0	0	0	0	0	0	0	0
1										
2										
3										
4										
5										
5										
6										
7										
8										
9										
End										

1C Create the Income Statement in the space provided below

Revenues	
Cost of Goods Sold	
Wage Expense	
Depreciation Expense	
Interest Expense	
Income Before Tax	
Tax Expense	
Net Income	

1A (continued)

9. Books $4 of Tax Expense to be paid later. (Use Tax Payable.)

Assets		Liabilities		Owners' Equity	
		4	Tax Pay.	(4)	Tax Exp.

1B Post the journal entries to the ledger. The Beginning Balances ("Begin") are all 0 because the firm is just commencing its business. Also note that Event 5 has two parts and is therefore listed twice in the ledger. Post revenue and all expenses directly to Retained Earnings.

	Assets				Liabilities and Owners' Equity					
	Cash	Inventory	Building	Total	Notes Payable	Interest Payable	Taxes Payable	Stock	Retained Earnings	Total
Begin	0	0	0	0	0	0	0	0	0	0
1	50				50					
2	20							20		
3	(30)		30							
4	(10)	10								
5	30								30	
5		(8)							(8)	
6	(2)								(2)	
7			(6)						(6)	
8						4			(4)	
9							4		(4)	
End	58	2	24	84	50	4	4	20	6	84

1C Create the Income Statement in the space provided below

Revenues	30
Cost of Goods Sold	(8)
Wage Expense	(2)
Depreciation Expense	(6)
Interest Expense	(4)
Income Before Tax	10
Tax Expense	(4)
Net Income	6

1D Label the Cash Flows in the Cash account (copied below) as Cash from Operations (CFO), Cash for Investing (CFI), or Cash from Financing (CFF). Also shown below are brief descriptions of the events to assist in the classifications.

	Cash	Description	Label
Begin	0		
1	50	Borrowed cash	
2	20	Sold stock	
3	(30)	Bought building	
4	(10)	Bought inventory	
5	30	Sold inventory	
5			
6	(2)	Paid employees	
7			
8			
9			
End	58		

1E Add up the cash flows by classification in the below space, and create the Statement of Cash Flows.

Statement of Cash Flows	
Cash from Operating Activities	
Cash used in Investing Activities	
Cash from Financing Activities	
Total Change in Cash	
Beginning Cash Balance	
Ending Cash Balance	

Congratulations. Your first "accounting cycle" is complete.

1D Label the Cash Flows in the Cash account (copied below) as Cash from Operations (CFO), Cash for Investing (CFI), or Cash from Financing (CFF). Also shown below are brief descriptions of the events to assist in the classifications.

	Cash	Description	Label
Begin	0		
1	50	Borrowed cash	CFF
2	20	Sold stock	CFF
3	(30)	Bought building	CFI
4	(10)	Bought inventory	CFO
5	30	Sold inventory	CFO
5			
6	(2)	Paid employees	CFO
7			
8			
9			
End	58		

1E Add up the cash flows by classification in the below space, and create the Statement of Cash Flows.

Statement of Cash Flows	
Cash from Operating Activities	18
Cash used in Investing Activities	(30)
Cash from Financing Activities	70
Total Change in Cash	58
Beginning Cash Balance	0
Ending Cash Balance	58

Congratulations. Your first "accounting cycle" is complete.

2   What do the initials "FASB" stand for?

3   What do the initials "IASB" stand for?

4   What do the initials "GAAP" stand for?

5   What is the fundamental accounting equation?

6   What is the purpose of the ledger?

7   What is the effect on Owners' Equity of booking a sale (increase, decrease, no effect)?

8   What is the effect on Owners' Equity of booking an expense (increase, decrease, no effect)?

9   What is the name of the account in Owners' Equity that contains a firm's Net Income?

10   What are the three main financial statements?

11   *True or False?* A Balance Sheet date could read "for the period ending 2009."

2   What do the initials "FASB" stand for?

Financial Accounting Standards Board

3   What do the initials "IASB" stand for?

International Accounting Standards Board

4   What do the initials "GAAP" stand for?

Generally Accepted Accounting Principles

5   What is the fundamental accounting equation?

Assets = Liabilities + Owners' Equity

6   What is the purpose of the ledger?

To collect data from journal entries and to show the balances for each account.

7   What is the effect on Owners' Equity of booking a sale (increase, decrease, no effect)?

Increase

8   What is the effect on Owners' Equity of booking an expense (increase, decrease, no effect)?

Decrease

9   What is the name of the account in Owners' Equity that contains a firm's Net Income?

Retained Earnings

10   What are the three main financial statements?

1. Balance Sheet
2. Income Statement
3. Statement of Cash Flows

11   *True or False?* A Balance Sheet date could read "for the period ending 2009."

False

12   *True or False?* An Income Statement date could read "as of 12/31/2009."

13   What are the names of the three types of cash flows shown on the cash flow statement?

14   What is the purpose of the closing entry?

12 *True or False?* An Income Statement date could read "as of 12/31/2009."

False

13 What are the names of the three types of cash flows shown on the cash flow statement?

1. Operating
2. Investing
3. Financing

14 What is the purpose of the closing entry?

To reset the balances of temporary accounts to zero and transfer data to Retained Earnings.

Practice Exercises

For use with Handbook Chapter 2

Practice Solutions

For use with Handbook Chapter 2

1 The below firm, called "Up and Running," is just going in to business.

1A Journalize the below transactions for Up and Running in the spaces provided. For each entry involving cash, label the cash flow as operating, CFO, investing, CFI, or financing, CFF.

1. **Up and Running issues (sells) its own stock for $100 cash. This is its "Initial Public Offering," or "IPO."**

Assets		Liabilities		Owners' Equity	
100	Cash			100	stock

2. **The firm borrows $50 cash.**

Assets		Liabilities		Owners' Equity	
50	Cash	50	Notes payable		

3. **Buys a building for $100 cash.**

Assets		Liabilities		Owners' Equity	
(100)	Cash				
B100	PP&E				

4. **Buys inventory for $50. It pays $40 cash. The remainder is on account. (Use Accounts Payable, A/P.)**

Assets		Liabilities		Owners' Equity	
(40)	Cash	10	A/P		
50	Inventory				

5. **Sells inventory costing $20 for $60. The sale is a credit sale.**

Assets		Liabilities		Owners' Equity	
60	A/R			60	sales
(20)	Inventory			(20)	COGS

6. **Collects $50 cash from the above Accounts Receivable, A/R.**

Assets		Liabilities		Owners' Equity	
50	Cash				
(50)	A/R				

7. **Records wage expense of $5 (Use Cash).**

Assets		Liabilities		Owners' Equity	
(5)	Cash			(5)	Wage

1 The below firm, called "Up and Running," is just going in to business.

1A Journalize the below transactions for Up and Running in the spaces provided. For each entry involving cash, label the cash flow as operating, CFO, investing, CFI, or financing, CFF.

1. Up and Running issues (sells) its own stock for $100 cash. This is its "Initial Public Offering," or "IPO."

Assets		Liabilities		Owners' Equity	
100	Cash CFF			100	Stock

2. The firm borrows $50 cash.

Assets		Liabilities		Owners' Equity	
50	Cash CFF	50	Note Pay.		

3. Buys a building for $100 cash.

Assets		Liabilities		Owners' Equity	
(100)	Cash CFI				
100	PP&E				

4. Buys inventory for $50. It pays $40 cash. The remainder is on account. (Use Accounts Payable, A/P.)

Assets		Liabilities		Owners' Equity	
50	Inventory	10	A/P		
(40)	Cash CFO				

5. Sells inventory costing $20 for $60. The sale is a credit sale.

Assets		Liabilities		Owners' Equity	
60	A/R			60	Sales
(20)	Inventory			(20)	COGS

6. Collects $50 cash from the above Accounts Receivable, A/R.

Assets		Liabilities		Owners' Equity	
50	Cash CFO				
(50)	A/R				

7. Records wage expense of $5 (Use Cash).

Assets		Liabilities		Owners' Equity	
(5)	Cash CFO			(5)	Wage Exp.

1A (continued)

8. Depreciates the building by $5. (Use the contra-account, Accumulated Depreciation, A/D.)

Assets		Liabilities		Owners' Equity	
(5)	A/D			(5)	DEP EX

9. Records $5 (or 10%) interest expense on the amount borrowed in 2. Will pay the interest later. (Use Interest Expense and Interest Payable.)

Assets		Liabilities		Owners' Equity	

10. Calculates tax expense as $10, which is 40% of pre-tax profit. Will pay the tax later. (Use Tax Expense and Tax Payable.)

Assets		Liabilities		Owners' Equity	

11. Up and Running closes its books. Use the space provided for the closing entry.

Assets		Liabilities		Owners' Equity	
					Sales
					COGS
					Wage Exp.
					Dep. Exp.
					Int. Exp.
					Tax. Exp.
					Ret. Earn.

1A   (continued)

8. Depreciates the building by $5. (Use the contra-account, Accumulated Depreciation, A/D.)

Assets		Liabilities		Owners' Equity	
(5)	A/D			(5)	Dep. Exp.

9. Records $5 (or 10%) interest expense on the amount borrowed in 2. Will pay the interest later. (Use Interest Expense and Interest Payable.)

Assets		Liabilities		Owners' Equity	
		5	Int. Pay.	(5)	Int. Exp.

10. Calculates tax expense as $10, which is 40% of pre-tax profit. Will pay the tax later. (Use Tax Expense and Tax Payable.)

Assets		Liabilities		Owners' Equity	
		10	Tax Pay.	(10)	Tax Exp.

11. Up and Running closes its books. Use the space provided for the closing entry.

Assets		Liabilities		Owners' Equity	
				(60)	Sales
				20	COGS
				5	Wage Exp.
				5	Dep. Exp.
				5	Int. Exp.
				10	Tax. Exp.
				15	Ret. Earn.

1B Post all of the above journal entries to the ledger below. All "Begin" balances are 0 because **Up and Running** is just starting business.

	Assets					Liabilities and Owners' Equity								Temporary Accounts					
	Cash	Accts. Rec.	Inventory	PP&E	A/D	Total	Accounts Payable	Interest Payable	Taxes Payable	Notes Payable	Stock	Retained Earnings	Total	Sales	COGS	Wage Expense	Dep. Exp.	Interest Exp.	Tax Exp.
Begin																			
1																			
2																			
3																			
4																			
5																			
6																			
7																			
8																			
9																			
10																			
11																			
End																			

1B Post all of the above journal entries to the ledger below. All "Begin" balances are 0 because **Up and Running** is just starting business.

	Assets						Liabilities and Owners' Equity							Temporary Accounts					
	Cash	Accts. Rec.	Inventory	PP&E	A/D	Total	Accounts Payable	Interest Payable	Taxes Payable	Notes Payable	Stock	Retained Earnings	Total	Sales	COGS	Wage Expense	Dep. Exp.	Interest Exp.	Tax Exp.
Begin	0	0	0	0	0	0	0	0	0	0	0	0	0	0	0	0	0	0	0
1	100										100								
2	50									50									
3	(100)			100															
4	(40)		50				10												
5		60	(20)											60	(20)				
6	50	(50)																	
7	(5)															(5)			
8					(5)												(5)		
9								5										(5)	
10									10			15							(10)
11												15		(60)	20	5	5	5	10
End	55	10	30	100	(5)	190	10	5	10	50	100	15	190	0	0	0	0	0	0

1C Fill in the values for the Income Statement below.

Sales	
Cost of Goods Sold	
Wage Expense	
Depreciation Expense	
Interest Expense	
Income Before Tax	
Income Tax Expense	
Net Income	

1D Aggregate the cash flows by category.

Cash from Operating Activities	
Cash used in Investing Activities	
Cash from Financing Activities	
Total change in Cash	

Congratulations. Your second "accounting cycle" is complete!

2 A firm buys office supplies for $100 cash.

2A Give the journal entry if the firm capitalizes the office supplies. (Use Office Supplies as the asset.)

Assets		Liabilities		Owners' Equity	

2B Give the journal entry if the firm expenses the office supplies. (Use SG&A Expense.)

Assets		Liabilities		Owners' Equity	

1C   Fill in the values for the Income Statement below.

Sales	60
Cost of Goods Sold	(20)
Wage Expense	(5)
Depreciation Expense	(5)
Interest Expense	(5)
Income Before Tax	25
Income Tax Expense	(10)
Net Income	15

1D   Aggregate the cash flows by category.

Cash from Operating Activities	5
Cash used in Investing Activities	(100)
Cash from Financing Activities	150
Total change in Cash	55

Congratulations. Your second "accounting cycle" is complete!

2   A firm buys office supplies for $100 cash.

2A   Give the journal entry if the firm capitalizes the office supplies. (Use Office Supplies as the asset.)

Assets		Liabilities		Owners' Equity	
(100)	Cash				
100	Office Supl.				

2B   Give the journal entry if the firm expenses the office supplies. (Use SG&A Expense.)

Assets		Liabilities		Owners' Equity	
(100)	Cash			(100)	SGA Exp.

---

3   A firm sells a car for $100 cash. The cost of the car is $80.

3A   If the firm is a car dealer and the sale of cars is its central activity, book the transaction.

Assets		Liabilities		Owners' Equity	

3B   If the firm does not normally sell cars but rather simply uses cars to visit customers, book the transaction. Assume that $80 is the car's net book value (cost less any accumulated depreciation). (Use Property, Plant, and Equipment, PP&E. That is, reduce PP&E by $80.)

Assets		Liabilities		Owners' Equity	

---

4   A firm reports the following Pre-Tax Income, Tax Expense, and Net Income.

Pre-Tax Income	150
Tax Expense	(40)
Net Income	110

What is the firm's Effective Tax Rate?

---

5   ***True or False?*** Tax free municipal bond interest will result in a firm's Effective Tax Rate being higher than the Statutory Tax Rate.

---

6   What are the 4 main steps of the accounting cycle?

---

7   What is the difference between revenues and gains?

---

3 A firm sells a car for $100 cash. The cost of the car is $80.

3A If the firm is a car dealer and the sale of cars is its central activity, book the transaction.

Assets		Liabilities		Owners' Equity	
100	Cash			100	Sale
(80)	Inventory			(80)	COGS

3B If the firm does not normally sell cars but rather simply uses cars to visit customers, book the transaction. Assume that $80 is the car's net book value (cost less any accumulated depreciation). (Use Property, Plant, and Equipment, PP&E. That is, reduce PP&E by $80.)

Assets		Liabilities		Owners' Equity	
100	Cash			20	Gain
(80)	PP&E				

4 A firm reports the following Pre-Tax Income, Tax Expense, and Net Income.

Pre-Tax Income	150
Tax Expense	(40)
Net Income	110

What is the firm's Effective Tax Rate?

27 %

5 ***True or False?*** Tax free municipal bond interest will result in a firm's Effective Tax Rate being higher than the Statutory Tax Rate.

False

6 What are the 4 main steps of the accounting cycle?

1. Identify
2. Value
3. Record
4. Disclose

7 What is the difference between revenues and gains?

Revenues are increases to Owners' Equity resulting from central, ongoing activities. Gains are increases to Owners' Equity resulting from peripheral activities.

Practice Exercises

For use with Handbook Chapter 3

Practice Solutions

For use with Handbook Chapter 3

1 Indicate which accounts go on the Income Statement, I/S, and which go on the Balance Sheet, B/S, by placing an "X" in the corresponding column.

	I/S	B/S
1. Accounts Receivable		
2. Accumulated Depreciation		
3. Cash		
4. Cost of Goods Sold		
5. Depreciation Expense		
6. Gain		
7. Income Tax Payable		
8. Interest Expense		
9. Interest Payable		
10. Inventory		
11. Investments		
12. Note Payable		
13. Prepaid Expense		
14. Property and Equipment		
15. Tax Expense		
16. R&D Expense		
17. Retained Earnings		
18. Revenue		
19. Salaries Expense		
20. Salaries Payable		
21. SG&A Expense		
22. Short Term Debt		
23. Stock		
24. Unearned Revenue		
25. Loss		

1 Indicate which accounts go on the Income Statement, I/S, and which go on the Balance Sheet, B/S, by placing an "X" in the corresponding column.

	I/S	B/S
1. Accounts Receivable		x
2. Accumulated Depreciation		x
3. Cash		x
4. Cost of Goods Sold	x	
5. Depreciation Expense	x	
6. Gain	x	
7. Income Tax Payable		x
8. Interest Expense	x	
9. Interest Payable		x
10. Inventory		x
11. Investments		x
12. Note Payable		x
13. Prepaid Expense		x
14. Property and Equipment		x
15. Tax Expense	x	
16. R&D Expense	x	
17. Retained Earnings		x
18. Revenue	x	
19. Salaries Expense	x	
20. Salaries Payable		x
21. SG&A Expense	x	
22. Short Term Debt		x
23. Stock		x
24. Unearned Revenue		x
25. Loss	x	

2

A firm prepays 2 years of insurance premiums on July 1, 2008. The amount paid was $24. The firm's Fiscal Year-end, FYE, is December 31. Give the journal entries on each of the below dates. Hint: first capitalize the payment of the premium as "Prepaid Expense." For the next 3 journal entries, pro-rate a portion of the "Prepaid Expense" to Insurance Expense based upon the respective amounts of time that have elapsed.

July 1, 2008

Assets		Liabilities		Owners' Equity	

December 31, 2008

Assets		Liabilities		Owners' Equity	

December 31, 2009

Assets		Liabilities		Owners' Equity	

June 30, 2010

Assets		Liabilities		Owners' Equity	

3

On January 1, 2008, a firm was paid $100 cash (upfront) by a customer for future services to be performed over the next 2 years. The firm's FYE is June 30. Give the firm's (not the customer's) journal entries on the below dates. Hint: First, the firm must defer the revenue because it has not earned it on January 1. By mid year, it will have earned a prorated amount.

January 1, 2008

Assets		Liabilities		Owners' Equity	

June 30, 2008

Assets		Liabilities		Owners' Equity	

Practice Exercises to
Accompany the FFAA Handbook | PART 2

2 A firm prepays 2 years of insurance premiums on July 1, 2008. The amount paid was $24. The firm's Fiscal Year-end, FYE, is December 31. Give the journal entries on each of the below dates. Hint: first capitalize the payment of the premium as "Prepaid Expense." For the next 3 journal entries, pro-rate a portion of the "Prepaid Expense" to Insurance Expense based upon the respective amounts of time that have elapsed.

July 1, 2008

Assets		Liabilities		Owners' Equity	
(24)	Cash				
24	Prepaid Exp.				

December 31, 2008

Assets		Liabilities		Owners' Equity	
(6)	Prepaid Exp.			(6)	Ins. Exp.

December 31, 2009

Assets		Liabilities		Owners' Equity	
(12)	Prepaid Exp.			(12)	Ins. Exp.

June 30, 2010

Assets		Liabilities		Owners' Equity	
(6)	Prepaid Exp.			(6)	Ins. Exp.

3 On January 1, 2008, a firm was paid $100 cash (upfront) by a customer for future services to be performed over the next 2 years. The firm's FYE is June 30. Give the firm's (not the customer's) journal entries on the below dates. Hint: First, the firm must defer the revenue because it has not earned it on January 1. By mid year, it will have earned a prorated amount.

January 1, 2008

Assets		Liabilities		Owners' Equity	
100	Cash	100	Unearn. Rev.		

June 30, 2008

Assets		Liabilities		Owners' Equity	
		(25)	Unearn. Rev.	25	Revenue

4 The below exercise will help internalize accounting vocabulary, such as accrue, defer, capitalize, expense. Give the journal entry for each event.

4A A firm defers revenue of $40.

Assets		Liabilities		Owners' Equity	

4B The firm earns $20 of the revenue deferred in **A**.

Assets		Liabilities		Owners' Equity	

4C The firm accrues expenses of $15. (Use Expense.)

Assets		Liabilities		Owners' Equity	

4D The firm pays $6 of the amount accrued in **C**.

Assets		Liabilities		Owners' Equity	

4E The firm prepays $7 of expenses. (Use Prepaid Expense.)

Assets		Liabilities		Owners' Equity	

4F The firm expenses $6 of the amount in **E**.

Assets		Liabilities		Owners' Equity	

4G The firm accrues $90 of revenue. (Use Accounts Receivable, A/R.)

Assets		Liabilities		Owners' Equity	

4H The firm collects $70 of the amount accrued in **G**.

Assets		Liabilities		Owners' Equity	

4   The below exercise will help internalize accounting vocabulary, such as accrue, defer, capitalize, expense. Give the journal entry for each event.

4A   A firm defers revenue of $40.

Assets		Liabilities		Owners' Equity	
40	Cash	40	Unearn. Rev.		

4B   The firm earns $20 of the revenue deferred in **A**.

Assets		Liabilities		Owners' Equity	
		(20)	Unearn. Rev.	20	Revenue

4C   The firm accrues expenses of $15. (Use Expense.)

Assets		Liabilities		Owners' Equity	
		15	Payable	(15)	Expense

4D   The firm pays $6 of the amount accrued in **C**.

Assets		Liabilities		Owners' Equity	
(6)	Cash	(6)	Payable		

4E   The firm prepays $7 of expenses. (Use Prepaid Expense.)

Assets		Liabilities		Owners' Equity	
(7)	Cash				
7	Prepaid Exp.				

4F   The firm expenses $6 of the amount in **E**.

Assets		Liabilities		Owners' Equity	
(6)	Prepaid Exp.			(6)	Expense

4G   The firm accrues $90 of revenue. (Use Accounts Receivable, A/R.)

Assets		Liabilities		Owners' Equity	
90	A/R			90	Revenue

4H   The firm collects $70 of the amount accrued in **G**.

Assets		Liabilities		Owners' Equity	
70	Cash				
(70)	A/R				

5 A firm is sued. The probable and estimable damages amount to $100. Under the conservatism principle, what journal entry would be required?

Assets		Liabilities		Owners' Equity	

6 A firm buys an investment for $40. The investment is a share of stock. The stock price increases to $44. Under fair value accounting, what journal entry would be required? (Journalize only the change in value, not the initial purchase of the investment. Use Unrealized Gain.)

Assets		Liabilities		Owners' Equity	

7 A firm has Net Income of $200 and has 100 shares of stock outstanding over the entire year. The firm has unexercised stock options that could add 40 more shares to the "share count" if the options were exercised.

7A What is Basic Earnings per Share, EPS?

7B What is Diluted EPS?

8 What are 4 phases of a firm's life cycle?

9 What do we normally expect to see in the "intro" and in the "growth" phases for the three categories of cash flows and for Net Income? (positive or negative will suffice)

	Intro	Growth
CFO		
CFI		
CFF		
Net Income		

10 Name an advantage of debt financing over equity financing.

5 A firm is sued. The probable and estimable damages amount to $100. Under the conservatism principle, what journal entry would be required?

Assets		Liabilities		Owners' Equity	
		100	Liability	(100)	Loss

6 A firm buys an investment for $40. The investment is a share of stock. The stock price increases to $44. Under fair value accounting, what journal entry would be required? (Journalize only the change in value, not the initial purchase of the investment. Use Unrealized Gain.)

Assets		Liabilities		Owners' Equity	
4	Investment			4	Unreal. Gain

7 A firm has Net Income of $200 and has 100 shares of stock outstanding over the entire year. The firm has unexercised stock options that could add 40 more shares to the "share count" if the options were exercised.

7A What is Basic Earnings per Share, EPS?

2.00

7B What is Diluted EPS?

1.43

8 What are 4 phases of a firm's life cycle?

1. Intro
2. Growth
3. Maturity
4. Decline

9 What do we normally expect to see in the "intro" and in the "growth" phases for the three categories of cash flows and for Net Income? (positive or negative will suffice)

	Intro	Growth
CFO	–	turns +
CFI	–	–
CFF	+	+
Net Income	–	turns +

10 Name an advantage of debt financing over equity financing.

Typically debt financing is cheaper.

11   Why is debt financing usually cheaper than equity financing?

12   True or False? Stockholders typically want the firm to take risks whereas debtholders do not.

13   What are Variable Operating Expenses?

14   State the revenue principle.

15   State the matching principle.

16   What is a stock option?

17   What is a stock option's strike price?

11 Why is debt financing usually cheaper than equity financing?

In the U.S., interest is generally deductible. Also debt can be less risky than equity, which makes the required returns to debtholders lower than those to equity holders. Debt can be less risky because debtholders typically hold collateral and have protective covenants.

12 True or False? Stockholders typically want the firm to take risks whereas debtholders do not.

True

13 What are Variable Operating Expenses?

These are operating expenses, such as COGS and SG&A Expense, that vary with sales.

14 State the revenue principle.

Revenue is booked when earned and realized or realizable.

15 State the matching principle.

Expenses are booked in the same period as the related revenues.

16 What is a stock option?

A stock option is a right that an option holder has to buy a share of stock at a predetermined price.

17 What is a stock option's strike price?

The strike price is the price that the option holder would pay to the firm to buy a share of stock. The option holder would be willing to exercise the option when the value of the stock is greater than the strike.

Practice Exercises

For use with Handbook Chapter 4

Practice Solutions

For use with Handbook Chapter 4

1

Assume a firm has an opening balance in its Accounts Receivable, A/R, account of $100. The firm subsequently makes $200 of credit sales, 10% of which are estimated to be uncollectible. The firm already has $15 in its Allowance for Bad Debt account (or minus $15, since this account has a negative balance). During the period, the firm collects $140 of the receivables. At the end of the current period, the firm "writes off" $12 of Accounts Receivable for customers who will not pay.

Journalize the following events.

1A The credit sales of $200.

Assets		Liabilities		Owners' Equity	

1B The additional amount of $20 (10% of $200) that is put in the Allowance for Bad Debt account for the above credit sales.

Assets		Liabilities		Owners' Equity	

1C The collection of cash of $140 from previous credit sales.

Assets		Liabilities		Owners' Equity	

1D The write off of $12.

Assets		Liabilities		Owners' Equity	

1E Using the schedule provided, calculate the Net Realizable Value of the Accounts Receivable.

Ending Balance in Accounts Receivable (Hint: start with the beginning balance and add or subtract as per above journal entries.)	
Ending Balance in Allowance for Bad Debt (Hint: same as above.)	
Net Realizable Value	

1 Assume a firm has an opening balance in its Accounts Receivable, A/R, account of $100. The firm subsequently makes $200 of credit sales, 10% of which are estimated to be uncollectible. The firm already has $15 in its Allowance for Bad Debt account (or minus $15, since this account has a negative balance). During the period, the firm collects $140 of the receivables. At the end of the current period, the firm "writes off" $12 of Accounts Receivable for customers who will not pay.

Journalize the following events.

1A The credit sales of $200.

Assets		Liabilities		Owners' Equity	
200	A/R			200	Sales

1B The additional amount of $20 (10% of $200) that is put in the Allowance for Bad Debt account for the above credit sales.

Assets		Liabilities		Owners' Equity	
(20)	Allowance			(20)	B.D. Expense

1C The collection of cash of $140 from previous credit sales.

Assets		Liabilities		Owners' Equity	
140	Cash				
(140)	A/R				

1D The write off of $12.

Assets		Liabilities		Owners' Equity	
(12)	A/R				
12	Allowance				

1E Using the schedule provided, calculate the Net Realizable Value of the Accounts Receivable.

Ending Balance in Accounts Receivable (Hint: start with the beginning balance and add or subtract as per above journal entries.)	148
Ending Balance in Allowance for Bad Debt (Hint: same as above.)	(23)
Net Realizable Value	125

2 A firm sells inventory to a customer for $1,000. The sale was a credit sale. The cost of the inventory sold (COGS) was $600. However, 1/4 of the sale was returned by the customer.

Journalize the following events from the firm's point of view, i.e. the seller's, not the customer's.

2A The credit sale of $1,000.

Assets		Liabilities		Owners' Equity	

2B The cost of the sale ($600).

Assets		Liabilities		Owners' Equity	

2C The reduction of the Account Receivable for the sales return. (Use "Sales Returns").

Assets		Liabilities		Owners' Equity	

2D The increase of the inventory for the sales return. (Hint: COGS will also be reduced, i.e. reversed.)

Assets		Liabilities		Owners' Equity	

2E What were the firm's Net Sales?

2F What was the firm's Net COGS?

2   A firm sells inventory to a customer for $1,000. The sale was a credit sale. The cost of the inventory sold (COGS) was $600. However, 1/4 of the sale was returned by the customer.

Journalize the following events from the firm's point of view, i.e. the seller's, not the customer's.

2A   The credit sale of $1,000.

Assets		Liabilities		Owners' Equity	
1,000	A/R			1,000	Sales

2B   The cost of the sale ($600).

Assets		Liabilities		Owners' Equity	
(600)	Inventory			(600)	COGS

2C   The reduction of the Account Receivable for the sales return. (Use "Sales Returns").

Assets		Liabilities		Owners' Equity	
(250)	A/R			(250)	Sales Ret.

2D   The increase of the inventory for the sales return. (Hint: COGS will also be reduced, i.e. reversed.)

Assets		Liabilities		Owners' Equity	
150	Inventory			150	COGS

2E   What were the firm's Net Sales?

750

2F   What was the firm's Net COGS?

(450)

3

Assume the following inventory data

	# units	cost ($/unit)
Beginning Inventory	1	20
Purchase #1	1	22
Purchase #2	1	24
Sale of Inventory	1	40
Ending Inventory in Units	2	

Goods Available For Sale, GAFS, are therefore $66 (20+22+24).

3A Fill in "Inventory" and "COGS" in the schedule below for each of the costing methods. Hint: GAFS = Inventory + COGS.

	GAFS	Inventory	COGS
FIFO	66		
Average	66		
LIFO	66		

3B Which of the above methods gives the highest Net Income?

4 What are the three inventory accounts for a manufacturer?

5 *True or False?* All depreciation is expensed immediately.

6 *True or False?* If ending inventory is overstated, Net Income will be overstated.

3

Assume the following inventory data

	# units	cost ($/unit)
Beginning Inventory	1	20
Purchase #1	1	22
Purchase #2	1	24
Sale of Inventory	1	40
Ending Inventory in Units	2	

Goods Available For Sale, GAFS, are therefore $66 (20+22+24).

3A Fill in "Inventory" and "COGS" in the schedule below for each of the costing methods. Hint: GAFS = Inventory + COGS.

	GAFS	Inventory	COGS
FIFO	66	46	20
Average	66	44	22
LIFO	66	42	24

3B Which of the above methods gives the highest Net Income?

FIFO, because it has the lowest COGS.

4 What are the three inventory accounts for a manufacturer?

1. Direct Materials

2. Work in Process

3. Finished Goods

5 *True or False?* All depreciation is expensed immediately.

False. Depreciation on manufacturing facilities and equipment is capitalized as part of inventory.

6 *True or False?* If ending inventory is overstated, Net Income will be overstated.

True. This is because if Ending Inventory is overstated, COGS is understated. The formula to see this is: Beginning Inventory + Purchases of Inventory = Ending Inventory + COGS. The left side of the above equation (which is GAFS) is a fixed amount. Thus, if "more" is assigned to Ending Inventory, "less" is assigned to COGS.

Practice Exercises

For use with Handbook Chapter 5

Practice Solutions

For use with Handbook Chapter 5

1   A firm buys the stock of another firm by paying $500 cash.

1A   Record the purchase of the stock.

Assets		Liabilities		Owners' Equity	

Assume that the firm (the Investor) has only a "passive interest" and also uses mark-to-market accounting. During the year after the acquisition, the stock price rises to $550.

1B   Record the increase in value assuming the Investor classifies the investment as "Trading". (Use an Unrealized Gain in the Income Statement.)

Assets		Liabilities		Owners' Equity	

1C   Record the increase in value assuming the Investor classifies the investment as "Available for Sale". (Use AOCI.)

Assets		Liabilities		Owners' Equity	

1D   Now assume that the firm (the Investor) has significant influence over the Investee through a 25% ownership stake. Also assume that the Investee has total income of $100. The Investor's share of the Investee's income is therefore $25 (25% * 100). Record the Investment Income for the Investor.

Assets		Liabilities		Owners' Equity	

1 A firm buys the stock of another firm by paying $500 cash.

1A Record the purchase of the stock.

Assets		Liabilities		Owners' Equity	
500	Investment				
(500)	Cash				

Assume that the firm (the Investor) has only a "passive interest" and also uses mark-to-market accounting. During the year after the acquisition, the stock price rises to $550.

1B Record the increase in value assuming the Investor classifies the investment as "Trading". (Use an Unrealized Gain in the Income Statement.)

Assets		Liabilities		Owners' Equity	
50	Investment			50	Unreal. Gain

1C Record the increase in value assuming the Investor classifies the investment as "Available for Sale". (Use AOCI.)

Assets		Liabilities		Owners' Equity	
50	Investment			50	AOCI

1D Now assume that the firm (the Investor) has significant influence over the Investee through a 25% ownership stake. Also assume that the Investee has total income of $100. The Investor's share of the Investee's income is therefore $25 (25% * 100). Record the Investment Income for the Investor.

Assets		Liabilities		Owners' Equity	
25	Investment			25	Inv. Income

Assume the following Balance Sheet for a firm that will be acquired by another firm.

	Book = Market
Cash	10
Inventory	20
Property, Plant, and Equipment	30
Total Assets	60
Liabilities	20
Stock	30
Retained Earnings	10
Total Liabilites and Owners' Equity	60

2

An acquirer purchases the above firm. The percentage purchased and the amount paid are below:

Percent purchased	100%
Price (all cash)	$ 60

2A Record the acquisition by the acquiring firm. Show the reduction in cash and the offsetting increase in an "Investment" account.

Assets		Liabilities		Owners' Equity	

2B Give the acquiring firm's "consolidation entry" to remove the "Investment" account and to consolidate the acquired firm's Balance Sheet. (Use Goodwill to make the journal entry balance!)

Assets		Liabilities		Owners' Equity	

Assume the following Balance Sheet for a firm that will be acquired by another firm.

	Book = Market
Cash	10
Inventory	20
Property, Plant, and Equipment	30
Total Assets	60
Liabilities	20
Stock	30
Retained Earnings	10
Total Liabilites and Owners' Equity	60

2

An acquirer purchases the above firm. The percentage purchased and the amount paid are below:

Percent purchased	100%
Price (all cash)	$ 60

2A Record the acquisition by the acquiring firm. Show the reduction in cash and the offsetting increase in an "Investment" account.

Assets		Liabilities		Owners' Equity	
(60)	Cash				
60	Investment				

2B Give the acquiring firm's "consolidation entry" to remove the "Investment" account and to consolidate the acquired firm's Balance Sheet. (Use Goodwill to make the journal entry balance!)

Assets		Liabilities		Owners' Equity	
(60)	Investment	20	Liabilities		
10	Cash				
20	Inventory				
30	PP&E				
20	Goodwill				

3 Which of the below long term assets are amortized or depreciated (yes) and which are not (no)?

	Yes or No?
Buildings	
Land	
Goodwill	
Patents purchased	
Trademarks to be renewed indefinitely	
Equipment	

4 A firm buys equipment from a manufacturer. The manufacturer also has a financing division that will finance the firm's purchase. The terms of the sale are that the firm must pay the manufacturer for the equipment in one year. The amount to be paid is $220, which includes $20 of interest.

4A Journalize this non-cash investing and financing transaction. (Use Equipment and Note Payable.)

Assets		Liabilities		Owners' Equity	

4B Journalize the firm's payment of the principal and interest to the manufacturer in one year.

Assets		Liabilities		Owners' Equity	

5 Assume that a firm spends $100 to build a building for its own use. This is a self-constructed asset. The firm also has debt of $500 that has an interest rate of 6%. Give the journal entry to book Interest Expense and the increase in the Building account for the amount of interest capitalized. The firm pays cash for the amount of interest it owes the bank.

Assets		Liabilities		Owners' Equity	

3　Which of the below long term assets are amortized or depreciated (yes) and which are not (no)?

	Yes or No?
Buildings	Yes
Land	No
Goodwill	No
Patents purchased	Yes
Trademarks to be renewed indefinitely	No
Equipment	Yes

4　A firm buys equipment from a manufacturer. The manufacturer also has a financing division that will finance the firm's purchase. The terms of the sale are that the firm must pay the manufacturer for the equipment in one year. The amount to be paid is $220, which includes $20 of interest.

4A　Journalize this non-cash investing and financing transaction. (Use Equipment and Note Payable.)

Assets		Liabilities		Owners' Equity	
200	Equipment	200	Note Payable		

4B　Journalize the firm's payment of the principal and interest to the manufacturer in one year.

Assets		Liabilities		Owners' Equity	
(220)	Cash	(200)	Note Payable	(20)	Interest Exp.

5　Assume that a firm spends $100 to build a building for its own use. This is a self-constructed asset. The firm also has debt of $500 that has an interest rate of 6%. Give the journal entry to book Interest Expense and the increase in the Building account for the amount of interest capitalized. The firm pays cash for the amount of interest it owes the bank.

Assets		Liabilities		Owners' Equity	
(30)	Cash			(24)	Interest Exp.
6	Building				

6 A firm buys equipment for $400. The residual value is expected to be $20, and the expected useful life is 10 years.

6A What is the depreciation expense for the first year and what is the book value of the equipment at the end of the first year using both of the below methods?

	Depreciation Expense	Book Value
Straight Line		
Double Declining Balance		

6B Give the journal entry for straight line depreciation assuming that the depreciation is appropriately expensed.

Assets		Liabilities		Owners' Equity	

6C Give the journal entry for straight line depreciation assuming that the depreciation is appropriately capitalized as part of inventory.

Assets		Liabilities		Owners' Equity	

6D If the firm sells the equipment after the first year for $350 cash, give the journal entry assuming that the firm had been using straight line depreciation for the year.

Assets		Liabilities		Owners' Equity	

6E If the firm sells the equipment after the first year for $350 cash, give the journal entry assuming that the firm had been using double declining balance depreciation for the year.

Assets		Liabilities		Owners' Equity	

6F *True or false?* Losses result when an asset is sold for less than its book value.

6	A firm buys equipment for $400. The residual value is expected to be $20, and the expected useful life is 10 years.

6A	What is the depreciation expense for the first year and what is the book value of the equipment at the end of the first year using both of the below methods?

	Depreciation Expense	Book Value
Straight Line	38	362
Double Declining Balance	80	320

6B	Give the journal entry for straight line depreciation assuming that the depreciation is appropriately expensed.

Assets		Liabilities		Owners' Equity	
(38)	A/D			(38)	Dep. Exp.

6C	Give the journal entry for straight line depreciation assuming that the depreciation is appropriately capitalized as part of inventory.

Assets		Liabilities		Owners' Equity	
(38)	A/D				
38	Inventory				

6D	If the firm sells the equipment after the first year for $350 cash, give the journal entry assuming that the firm had been using straight line depreciation for the year.

Assets		Liabilities		Owners' Equity	
350	Cash			(12)	Loss
(400)	Equipment				
38	A/D				

6E	If the firm sells the equipment after the first year for $350 cash, give the journal entry assuming that the firm had been using double declining balance depreciation for the year.

Assets		Liabilities		Owners' Equity	
350	Cash			30	Gain
(400)	Equipment				
80	A/D				

6F	**_True or false?_** Losses result when an asset is sold for less than its book value.

True

7 Assume that a firm has equipment that costs $400 and has a 10 year useful life. After 3 years of straight line depreciation (and no residual value), Accumulated Depreciation is $120. The firm estimates that the fair value of the equipment has fallen to $200 and is likely not to recover in value.

Journalize the impairment of the equipment.

Assets		Liabilities		Owners' Equity	

7

Assume that a firm has equipment that costs $400 and has a 10 year useful life. After 3 years of straight line depreciation (and no residual value), Accumulated Depreciation is $120. The firm estimates that the fair value of the equipment has fallen to $200 and is likely not to recover in value.

Journalize the impairment of the equipment.

Assets		Liabilities		Owners' Equity	
(80)	Equipment			(80)	Impair. Loss

Practice Exercises

For use with Handbook Chapter 6

Practice Solutions

For use with Handbook Chapter 6

1 A firm borrows money from a bank. The bank requires the firm to pay both principal and interest in 2 years in the combined amount of $1,000. The bank charges 6% interest on all loans. This is an accreting loan because no payments are made until the due date in 2 years.

1A How much will the bank loan the firm? (Round to the nearest dollar amount.) Hint: solve for the present value of the $1,000 that is due in 2 years.

1B What will be the balance of the bank loan after one year? An accretion table is set up below to facilitate the calculation.

Cash Payment	Interest	Principal Adjustment	Principal Balance	
	6%			← Present value
0				← Balance after 1 year
0				← Future value

2 A firm borrows money from a bank. The bank requires the firm to make 2, $1,000 payments at the end of each of the next 2 years. The bank charges 6% interest on all loans. Each payment will be for part interest and part principal; therefore, the loan is an amortizing loan.

2A How much will the bank loan the firm? (Round to the nearest dollar amount.) Hint: solve for the present value of the 2 year annuity of $1,000, using the 6% interest rate.

2B What will be the balance of the bank loan after one year? An amortization table is set up below to facilitate the calculation.

Cash Payment	Interest	Principal Adjustment	Principal Balance	
	6%			← Present value
1,000				← Balance after 1 year
1,000				← Future value

3 A firm leases a building. The lease qualifies as a capital lease. The lease payments are $100 for 2 years, at the end of each year. The appropriate interest rate is 10%.

3A Journalize the inception of the lease. Hint: solve for the present value of the 2 year annuity of $100, using the 10% interest rate.

Assets		Liabilities		Owners' Equity	

1 A firm borrows money from a bank. The bank requires the firm to pay both principal and interest in 2 years in the combined amount of $1,000. The bank charges 6% interest on all loans. This is an accreting loan because no payments are made until the due date in 2 years.

1A How much will the bank loan the firm? (Round to the nearest dollar amount.) Hint: solve for the present value of the $1,000 that is due in 2 years.

> 890

1B What will be the balance of the bank loan after one year? An accretion table is set up below to facilitate the calculation.

Cash Payment	Interest	Principal Adjustment	Principal Balance	
	6%		890	← Present value
0	53	53	943	← Balance after 1 year
0	57	57	1,000	← Future value

2 A firm borrows money from a bank. The bank requires the firm to make 2, $1,000 payments at the end of each of the next 2 years. The bank charges 6% interest on all loans. Each payment will be for part interest and part principal; therefore, the loan is an amortizing loan.

2A How much will the bank loan the firm? (Round to the nearest dollar amount.) Hint: solve for the present value of the 2 year annuity of $1,000, using the 6% interest rate.

> 1,833

2B What will be the balance of the bank loan after one year? An amortization table is set up below to facilitate the calculation.

Cash Payment	Interest	Principal Adjustment	Principal Balance	
	6%		1,833	← Present value
1,000	110	890	943	← Balance after 1 year
1,000	57	943	0	← Future value

3 A firm leases a building. The lease qualifies as a capital lease. The lease payments are $100 for 2 years, at the end of each year. The appropriate interest rate is 10%.

3A Journalize the inception of the lease. Hint: solve for the present value of the 2 year annuity of $100, using the 10% interest rate.

Assets		Liabilities		Owners' Equity	
174	Asset	174	Liability		

3B Set up an amortization table for the liability.

Cash Payment	Interest	Principal Adjustment	Principal Balance	
	10%			← Present value
100				
100				← Future value

4 Assume that the above lease is an operating lease.

4A What journal entry, if any, would the firm make at the inception of the lease?

Assets		Liabilities		Owners' Equity	

4B What journal entry would the firm make at the end of the first year of the lease? (Use SG&A Expense.)

Assets		Liabilities		Owners' Equity	

5 Assume a firm issues a bond with a face value of $1,000. The stated rate of interest is 4%. The market rate of interest is 7%. The maturity is in 2 years. Interest is paid yearly.

5A Journalize the bond issue. Hint: solve for the present value of all cash flows, both the 2 year annuity and the maturity value of $1,000. Use 4% to calculate the annuity and use 7% as the discount rate to solve for the present value.

Assets		Liabilities		Owners' Equity	

5B Complete the amortization table for the bond.

Cash Payment	Interest	Principal Adjustment	Principal Balance	
	7%			← Present value
40				
40				← Future value

3B   Set up an amortization table for the liability.

Cash Payment	Interest	Principal Adjustment	Principal Balance	
	10%		174	← Present value
100	17	83	91	
100	9	91	0	← Future value

4   Assume that the above lease is an operating lease.

4A   What journal entry, if any, would the firm make at the inception of the lease?

Assets		Liabilities		Owners' Equity	
No Entry		No Entry		No Entry	

4B   What journal entry would the firm make at the end of the first year of the lease? (Use SG&A Expense.)

Assets		Liabilities		Owners' Equity	
(100)	Cash			(100)	SG&A Exp.

5   Assume a firm issues a bond with a face value of $1,000. The stated rate of interest is 4%. The market rate of interest is 7%. The maturity is in 2 years. Interest is paid yearly.

5A   Journalize the bond issue. Hint: solve for the present value of all cash flows, both the 2 year annuity and the maturity value of $1,000. Use 4% to calculate the annuity and use 7% as the discount rate to solve for the present value.

Assets		Liabilities		Owners' Equity	
946	Cash	946	Bond Pay.		

5B   Complete the amortization table for the bond.

Cash Payment	Interest	Principal Adjustment	Principal Balance	
	7%		946	← Present value
40	66	26	972	
40	68	28	1,000	← Future value

6 Assume a firm issues a bond with a face value of $1,000. The stated rate of interest is 7%. The market rate of interest is 4%. The maturity is in 2 years. Interest is paid yearly.

6A Journalize the bond issue. Hint: solve for the present value of all cash flows, both the 2 year annuity and the maturity value of $1,000. Use 7% to calculate the annuity and use 4% as the discount rate to solve for the present value.

Assets		Liabilities		Owners' Equity	

6B Complete the amortization table for the bond.

Cash Payment	Interest	Principal Adjustment	Principal Balance	
	4%			← Present value
70				
70				← Future value

7 Place a check in the proper cells below for the cause of the respective tax positions. Specifically, which is associated with Deferred Tax Assets, DTAs, and Deferred Tax Liabilities, DTLs: "accelerated" deductions or "deferred" deductions?

	Accelerated	Deferred
DTA		
DTL		

8 True or False? Deferred Tax Liabilities are recognized in the Balance Sheet at the present value of cash payments.

9 Assume a firm declares a total cash dividend of $50. Payment will be made at a later date.

9A Give the journal entry on the declaration date. Hint: reduce Retained Earnings directly.

Assets		Liabilities		Owners' Equity	

9B Give the journal entry on the payment date.

Assets		Liabilities		Owners' Equity	

| 6 | Assume a firm issues a bond with a face value of $1,000. The stated rate of interest is 7%. The market rate of interest is 4%. The maturity is in 2 years. Interest is paid yearly. |

| 6A | Journalize the bond issue. Hint: solve for the present value of all cash flows, both the 2 year annuity and the maturity value of $1,000. Use 7% to calculate the annuity and use 4% as the discount rate to solve for the present value. |

Assets		Liabilities		Owners' Equity	
1,057	Cash	1,057	Bond Pay.		

6B Complete the amortization table for the bond.

Cash Payment	Interest	Principal Adjustment	Principal Balance	
	4%		1,057	← Present value
70	42	28	1,029	
70	41	29	1,000	← Future value

| 7 | Place a check in the proper cells below for the cause of the respective tax positions. Specifically, which is associated with Deferred Tax Assets, DTAs, and Deferred Tax Liabilities, DTLs: "accelerated" deductions or "deferred" deductions? |

	Accelerated	Deferred
DTA		x
DTL	x	

| 8 | ***True or False?*** Deferred Tax Liabilities are recognized in the Balance Sheet at the present value of cash payments. |

| False |

| 9 | Assume a firm declares a total cash dividend of $50. Payment will be made at a later date. |

9A Give the journal entry on the declaration date. Hint: reduce Retained Earnings directly.

Assets		Liabilities		Owners' Equity	
		50	Div. Payable	(50)	Ret. Earnings

9B Give the journal entry on the payment date.

Assets		Liabilities		Owners' Equity	
(50)	Cash	(50)	Div. Payable		

Assume that the above firm has 20 shares of Preferred Stock outstanding, each with a $5 par value. The preferred stock's dividend rate is 6%.

9C   How much of the $50 dividend will go to the Preferred Shareholders?

9D   How much of the $50 dividend will go to the Common Shareholders?

10   Journalize the following transactions.

10A A firm issues 10 shares of $3 par value Common Stock for $20 per share. Hint: put only the total "par value" in the Common Stock account. The remainder goes into "Additional Paid in Capital", APIC.

Assets		Liabilities		Owners' Equity	

10B The firm buys back 2 shares for $30 per share. (Use Treasury Stock.)

Assets		Liabilities		Owners' Equity	

10C The firm sells 1 of the treasury shares for $50 per share. Hint: remember that no gains or losses are booked on Treasury Stock sales.

Assets		Liabilities		Owners' Equity	

10D The firm sells the other treasury share for $25 per share.

Assets		Liabilities		Owners' Equity	

Assume that the above firm has 20 shares of Preferred Stock outstanding, each with a $5 par value. The preferred stock's dividend rate is 6%.

9C   How much of the $50 dividend will go to the Preferred Shareholders?

> 6

9D   How much of the $50 dividend will go to the Common Shareholders?

> 44

10   Journalize the following transactions.

10A   A firm issues 10 shares of $3 par value Common Stock for $20 per share. Hint: put only the total "par value" in the Common Stock account. The remainder goes into "Additional Paid in Capital", APIC.

Assets		Liabilities		Owners' Equity	
200	Cash			30	Stock
				170	APIC

10B   The firm buys back 2 shares for $30 per share. (Use Treasury Stock.)

Assets		Liabilities		Owners' Equity	
(60)	Cash			(60)	Treas. Stock

10C   The firm sells 1 of the treasury shares for $50 per share. Hint: remember that no gains or losses are booked on Treasury Stock sales.

Assets		Liabilities		Owners' Equity	
50	Cash			30	Treas. Stock
				20	APIC

10D   The firm sells the other treasury share for $25 per share.

Assets		Liabilities		Owners' Equity	
25	Cash			30	Treas. Stock
				(5)	APIC

Practice Exercises

For use with Handbook Chapter 7

Practice Solutions

For use with Handbook Chapter 7

| **1** | What is the accounting classification (under U.S. GAAP) for each of the below cash flows (CFO, CFI, or CFF)? |

a. Cash received from customers.	
b. Cash paid to suppliers of inventory.	
c. Cash paid for a building.	
d. Cash received from stockholders upon the sale of the firm's stock.	
e. Cash paid to stockholders in the form of a dividend.	
f. Cash paid to stockholders to buy back their stock.	
g. Cash received from the sale of a building.	
h. Cash received from a bank as a loan.	
i. Cash paid to employees as salaries and wages.	
j. Cash paid to the utility company for electricity.	
k. Cash paid to the government for taxes.	
l. Cash paid to the bank as interest on a loan.	
m. Cash paid to the bank as principal repayment.	
n. Cash received as interest on an investment in a bond.	
o. Cash received as a dividend on an investment in stock.	

| **2** | If a firm's beginning and ending balances in Accounts Receivable are $100 and 120, respectively, and if credit sales were $180, what is the amount of cash collected, assuming no other activity in the receivables account? |

Beginning	Credit Sales	Cash	Ending
100	180		120

| **3** | If a firm's beginning and ending balances in Accrued Expenses (such as wages or salaries) are $50 and $40, respectively, and if the related SG&A Expense was $20, how much cash was paid for these expenses? |

Beginning	Expense	Cash	Ending
50	20		40

| **4** | If a firm's beginning and ending balances in Retained Earnings are $80 and 90, respectively, and if Net Income was $50, what were "Dividends Declared" assuming no other activity in Retained Earnings? |

Beginning	Net Income	Dividends Declared	Ending
80	50		90

1   What is the accounting classification (under U.S. GAAP) for each of the below cash flows (CFO, CFI, or CFF)?

a. Cash received from customers.	CFO
b. Cash paid to suppliers of inventory.	CFO
c. Cash paid for a building.	CFI
d. Cash received from stockholders upon the sale of the firm's stock.	CFF
e. Cash paid to stockholders in the form of a dividend.	CFF
f. Cash paid to stockholders to buy back their stock.	CFF
g. Cash received from the sale of a building.	CFI
h. Cash received from a bank as a loan.	CFF
i. Cash paid to employees as salaries and wages.	CFO
j. Cash paid to the utility company for electricity.	CFO
k. Cash paid to the government for taxes.	CFO
l. Cash paid to the bank as interest on a loan.	CFO
m. Cash paid to the bank as principal repayment.	CFF
n. Cash received as interest on an investment in a bond.	CFO
o. Cash received as a dividend on an investment in stock.	CFO

2   If a firm's beginning and ending balances in Accounts Receivable are $100 and 120, respectively, and if credit sales were $180, what is the amount of cash collected, assuming no other activity in the receivables account?

Beginning	Credit Sales	Cash	Ending
100	180	(160)	120

3   If a firm's beginning and ending balances in Accrued Expenses (such as wages or salaries) are $50 and $40, respectively, and if the related SG&A Expense was $20, how much cash was paid for these expenses?

Beginning	Expense	Cash	Ending
50	20	(30)	40

4   If a firm's beginning and ending balances in Retained Earnings are $80 and 90, respectively, and if Net Income was $50, what were "Dividends Declared" assuming no other activity in Retained Earnings?

Beginning	Net Income	Dividends Declared	Ending
80	50	(40)	90

5 If a firm's beginning and ending balances in Inventory are $10 and 12, respectively, and if COGS was $20, how much Inventory was purchased?

Beginning	Purchases	COGS	Ending
10		(20)	12

Problems 6–9 require us to derive the Statement of Cash Flows using the Indirect Method for CFO. Schedules are included to facilitate the calculations:

- Problem 6 is straightforward, with no gains, losses, and dividends.

- Problem 7 introduces a dividend.

- Problem 8 introduces a gain and we need to follow the instructions to calculate the amount of cash received on the sale of the Investment.

- Problem 9 is similar to Problem 8, but the Investment is sold for a loss.

5 If a firm's beginning and ending balances in Inventory are $10 and 12, respectively, and if COGS was $20, how much Inventory was purchased?

Beginning	Purchases	COGS	Ending
10	22	(20)	12

Problems 6–9 require us to derive the Statement of Cash Flows using the Indirect Method for CFO. Schedules are included to facilitate the calculations:

- Problem 6 is straightforward, with no gains, losses, and dividends.

- Problem 7 introduces a dividend.

- Problem 8 introduces a gain and we need to follow the instructions to calculate the amount of cash received on the sale of the Investment.

- Problem 9 is similar to Problem 8, but the Investment is sold for a loss.

6   Derive the firm's Statement of Cash Flows

Income Statement	
Sales	180
Cost of Goods Sold	(90)
Depreciation Expense	(10)
Interest Expense	(10)
Income Before Tax	70
Income Tax Expense	(28)
Net Income	42
Dividends	0

Balance Sheet	Previous Year	Current Year	Change
Cash	58	80	22
Accounts Receivable	32	50	18
Inventory	35	50	15
Investment	20	12	(8)
PP&E	130	150	20
Accumulated Deprecation	(50)	(60)	(10)
Total Assets	225	282	57
Accounts Payable	30	38	8
Income Tax Payable	15	8	(7)
Notes Payable	100	120	20
Stock	40	40	0
Retained Earnings	40	82	42
Treasury Stock	0	(6)	(6)
Total Liabilities & Owners' Equity	225	282	57

Statement of Cash Flows	
Net Income	
Depreciation Expense	
Change in Accounts Receivable	
Change in Inventory	
Change in Accounts Payable	
Change in Tax Payable	
CFO	
Sale of Investment	
Change in PP&E	
CFI	
Change in Notes Payable	
Repurchase of Stock	
CFF	
Total Change in Cash	
Beginning Cash	
Ending Cash	

6   Derive the firm's Statement of Cash Flows

Income Statement	
Sales	180
Cost of Goods Sold	(90)
Depreciation Expense	(10)
Interest Expense	(10)
Income Before Tax	70
Income Tax Expense	(28)
Net Income	42
Dividends	0

Balance Sheet	Previous Year	Current Year	Change
Cash	58	80	22
Accounts Receivable	32	50	18
Inventory	35	50	15
Investment	20	12	(8)
PP&E	130	150	20
Accumulated Deprecation	(50)	(60)	(10)
Total Assets	225	282	57
Accounts Payable	30	38	8
Income Tax Payable	15	8	(7)
Notes Payable	100	120	20
Stock	40	40	0
Retained Earnings	40	82	42
Treasury Stock	0	(6)	(6)
Total Liabilities & Owners' Equity	225	282	57

Statement of Cash Flows	
Net Income	42
Depreciation Expense	10
Change in Accounts Receivable	(18)
Change in Inventory	(15)
Change in Accounts Payable	8
Change in Tax Payable	(7)
CFO	20
Sale of Investment	8
Change in PP&E	(20)
CFI	(12)
Change in Notes Payable	20
Repurchase of Stock	(6)
CFF	14
Total Change in Cash	22
Beginning Cash	58
Ending Cash	80

7 Derive the firm's Statement of Cash Flows

Income Statement	
Sales	180
Cost of Goods Sold	(90)
Depreciation Expense	(10)
Interest Expense	(10)
Income Before Tax	70
Income Tax Expense	(28)
Net Income	42
Dividends	6

Balance Sheet	Previous Year	Current Year	Change
Cash	58	74	16
Accounts Receivable	32	50	18
Inventory	35	50	15
Investment	20	12	(8)
PP&E	130	150	20
Accumulated Deprecation	(50)	(60)	(10)
Total Assets	225	276	51
Accounts Payable	30	38	8
Income Tax Payable	15	8	(7)
Notes Payable	100	120	20
Stock	40	40	0
Retained Earnings	40	76	36
Treasury Stock	0	(6)	(6)
Total Liabilities & Owners' Equity	225	276	51

Statement of Cash Flows	
Net Income	
Depreciation Expense	
Change in Accounts Receivable	
Change in Inventory	
Change in Accounts Payable	
Change in Tax Payable	
CFO	
Sale of Investment	
Change in PP&E	
CFI	
Change in Notes Payable	
Repurchase of Stock	
Dividends	
CFF	
Total Change in Cash	
Beginning Cash	
Ending Cash	

7   Derive the firm's Statement of Cash Flows

Income Statement	
Sales	180
Cost of Goods Sold	(90)
Depreciation Expense	(10)
Interest Expense	(10)
Income Before Tax	70
Income Tax Expense	(28)
Net Income	42
Dividends	6

Balance Sheet	Previous Year	Current Year	Change
Cash	58	74	16
Accounts Receivable	32	50	18
Inventory	35	50	15
Investment	20	12	(8)
PP&E	130	150	20
Accumulated Deprecation	(50)	(60)	(10)
Total Assets	225	276	51
Accounts Payable	30	38	8
Income Tax Payable	15	8	(7)
Notes Payable	100	120	20
Stock	40	40	0
Retained Earnings	40	76	36
Treasury Stock	0	(6)	(6)
Total Liabilities & Owners' Equity	225	276	51

Statement of Cash Flows	
Net Income	42
Depreciation Expense	10
Change in Accounts Receivable	(18)
Change in Inventory	(15)
Change in Accounts Payable	8
Change in Tax Payable	(7)
CFO	20
Sale of Investment	8
Change in PP&E	(20)
CFI	(12)
Change in Notes Payable	20
Repurchase of Stock	(6)
Dividends	(6)
CFF	8
Total Change in Cash	16
Beginning Cash	58
Ending Cash	74

8   Derive the firm's Statement of Cash Flows

Income Statement	
Sales	180
Cost of Goods Sold	(90)
Depreciation Expense	(10)
Interest Expense	(10)
Gain	5
Income Before Tax	75
Income Tax Expense	(30)
Net Income	45
Dividends	6

An investment that cost $8 was sold for a gain of $5. Do a transaction analysis in the space below to determine the amount of cash received. Label the cash flow as CFI.

Assets		Liabilities		Owners' Equity	

Balance Sheet	Previous Year	Current Year	Change
Cash	58	77	19
Accounts Receivable	32	50	18
Inventory	35	50	15
Investment	20	12	(8)
PP&E	130	150	20
Accumulated Deprecation	(50)	(60)	(10)
Total Assets	225	279	54
Accounts Payable	30	38	8
Income Tax Payable	15	8	(7)
Notes Payable	100	120	20
Stock	40	40	0
Retained Earnings	40	79	39
Treasury Stock	0	(6)	(6)
Total Liabilities & Owners' Equity	225	279	54

Statement of Cash Flows	
Net Income	
Depreciation Expense	
Gain	
Change in Accounts Receivable	
Change in Inventory	
Change in Accounts Payable	
Change in Tax Payable	
CFO	
Sale of Investment	
Change in PP&E	
CFI	
Change in Notes Payable	
Repurchase of Stock	
Dividends	
CFF	
Total Change in Cash	
Beginning Cash	
Ending Cash	

8 Derive the firm's Statement of Cash Flows

Income Statement	
Sales	180
Cost of Goods Sold	(90)
Depreciation Expense	(10)
Interest Expense	(10)
Gain	5
Income Before Tax	75
Income Tax Expense	(30)
Net Income	45
Dividends	6

An investment that cost $8 was sold for a gain of $5. Do a transaction analysis in the space below to determine the amount of cash received. Label the cash flow as CFI.

Assets		Liabilities		Owners' Equity	
13	Cash CFI				
(8)	Investment			5	Gain

Balance Sheet	Previous Year	Current Year	Change
Cash	58	77	19
Accounts Receivable	32	50	18
Inventory	35	50	15
Investment	20	12	(8)
PP&E	130	150	20
Accumulated Deprecation	(50)	(60)	(10)
Total Assets	225	279	54
Accounts Payable	30	38	8
Income Tax Payable	15	8	(7)
Notes Payable	100	120	20
Stock	40	40	0
Retained Earnings	40	79	39
Treasury Stock	0	(6)	(6)
Total Liabilities & Owners' Equity	225	279	54

Statement of Cash Flows	
Net Income	45
Depreciation Expense	10
Gain	(5)
Change in Accounts Receivable	(18)
Change in Inventory	(15)
Change in Accounts Payable	8
Change in Tax Payable	(7)
CFO	18
Sale of Investment	13
Change in PP&E	(20)
CFI	(7)
Change in Notes Payable	20
Repurchase of Stock	(6)
Dividends	(6)
CFF	8
Total Change in Cash	19
Beginning Cash	58
Ending Cash	77

9 | Derive the firm's Statement of Cash Flows

Income Statement	
Sales	180
Cost of Goods Sold	(90)
Depreciation Expense	(10)
Interest Expense	(10)
Loss	(5)
Income Before Tax	65
Income Tax Expense	(26)
Net Income	39
Dividends	6

An investment that cost $8 was sold for a loss of $5. Do a transaction analysis in the space below to determine the amount of cash received. Label the cash flow as CFI.

Assets		Liabilities		Owners' Equity	

Balance Sheet	Previous Year	Current Year	Change
Cash	58	71	13
Accounts Receivable	32	50	18
Inventory	35	50	15
Investment	20	12	(8)
PP&E	130	150	20
Accumulated Deprecation	(50)	(60)	(10)
Total Assets	225	273	48
Accounts Payable	30	38	8
Income Tax Payable	15	8	(7)
Notes Payable	100	120	20
Stock	40	40	0
Retained Earnings	40	73	33
Treasury Stock	0	(6)	(6)
Total Liabilities & Owners' Equity	225	273	48

Statement of Cash Flows	
Net Income	
Depreciation Expense	
Loss	
Change in Accounts Receivable	
Change in Inventory	
Change in Accounts Payable	
Change in Tax Payable	
CFO	
Sale of Investment	
Change in PP&E	
CFI	
Change in Notes Payable	
Repurchase of Stock	
Dividends	
CFF	
Total Change in Cash	
Beginning Cash	
Ending Cash	

9 Derive the firm's Statement of Cash Flows

Income Statement	
Sales	180
Cost of Goods Sold	(90)
Depreciation Expense	(10)
Interest Expense	(10)
Loss	(5)
Income Before Tax	65
Income Tax Expense	(26)
Net Income	39
Dividends	6

An investment that cost $8 was sold for a loss of $5. Do a transaction analysis in the space below to determine the amount of cash received. Label the cash flow as CFI.

Assets		Liabilities		Owners' Equity	
3	Cash CFI				
(8)	Investment			(5)	Loss

Balance Sheet	Previous Year	Current Year	Change
Cash	58	71	13
Accounts Receivable	32	50	18
Inventory	35	50	15
Investment	20	12	(8)
PP&E	130	150	20
Accumulated Deprecation	(50)	(60)	(10)
Total Assets	225	273	48
Accounts Payable	30	38	8
Income Tax Payable	15	8	(7)
Notes Payable	100	120	20
Stock	40	40	0
Retained Earnings	40	73	33
Treasury Stock	0	(6)	(6)
Total Liabilities & Owners' Equity	225	273	48

Statement of Cash Flows	
Net Income	39
Depreciation Expense	10
Loss	5
Change in Accounts Receivable	(18)
Change in Inventory	(15)
Change in Accounts Payable	8
Change in Tax Payable	(7)
CFO	22
Sale of Investment	3
Change in PP&E	(20)
CFI	(17)
Change in Notes Payable	20
Repurchase of Stock	(6)
Dividends	(6)
CFF	8
Total Change in Cash	13
Beginning Cash	58
Ending Cash	71

137

Practice Exercises

For use with Handbook Chapter 8

Practice Solutions

For use with Handbook Chapter 8

1 Below are a firm's Income Statement and comparative Balance Sheets.

Income Statement	
Sales	200
Cost of Goods Sold	(120)
SG&A Expense	(60)
Depreciation Expense	(6)
Interest Expense	(4)
Income Before Tax	10
Income Tax Expense	(4)
Net Income	6
Dividends	2

1A Calculate the missing Year-over-Year, YOY, and Common Size, CS, ratios.

Balance Sheet	Previous Year	Current Year	YOY	Previous Year CS	Current Year CS
Cash	10	13		0.07	0.09
Accounts Receivable	30	25		0.20	0.18
Inventory	20	10	(0.50)		
PP&E	100	110	0.10		
Accumulated Depreciation	(10)	(16)	0.60	(0.07)	(0.11)
Total Assets	150	142	(0.05)	1.00	1.00
Accounts Payable	20	15	(0.25)	0.13	0.11
Notes Payable	60	60	0.00		
Stock	20	20	0.00	0.13	0.14
Retained Earnings	50	54		0.33	0.38
Treasury Stock	0	(7)	n/a	0.00	(0.05)
Total Liabilities & Owners' Equity	150	142	(0.05)	1.00	1.00

1   Below are a firm's Income Statement and comparative Balance Sheets.

Income Statement	
Sales	200
Cost of Goods Sold	(120)
SG&A Expense	(60)
Depreciation Expense	(6)
Interest Expense	(4)
Income Before Tax	10
Income Tax Expense	(4)
Net Income	6
Dividends	2

1A   Calculate the missing Year-over-Year, YOY, and Common Size, CS, ratios.

Balance Sheet	Previous Year	Current Year	YOY	Previous Year CS	Current Year CS
Cash	10	13	0.30	0.07	0.09
Accounts Receivable	30	25	(0.17)	0.20	0.18
Inventory	20	10	(0.50)	0.13	0.07
PP&E	100	110	0.10	0.67	0.77
Accumulated Depreciation	(10)	(16)	0.60	(0.07)	(0.11)
Total Assets	150	142	(0.05)	1.00	1.00
Accounts Payable	20	15	(0.25)	0.13	0.11
Notes Payable	60	60	0.00	0.40	0.42
Stock	20	20	0.00	0.13	0.14
Retained Earnings	50	54	0.08	0.33	0.38
Treasury Stock	0	(7)	n/a	0.00	(0.05)
Total Liabilities & Owners' Equity	150	142	(0.05)	1.00	1.00

1B Derive the firm's Statement of Cash Flows.

Statement of Cash Flows	
CFO	
Net Income	
Depreciation Expense	
Change in Accounts Receivable	
Change in Inventory	
Change in Accounts Payable	
Total	
CFI	
Change in PP&E	
CFF	
Repurchases of Stock	
Dividends	
Total CFF	
Total Change in Cash	
Beginning Cash	
Ending Cash	

1B   Derive the firm's Statement of Cash Flows.

Statement of Cash Flows	
CFO	
Net Income	6
Depreciation Expense	6
Change in Accounts Receivable	5
Change in Inventory	10
Change in Accounts Payable	(5)
Total	22
CFI	
Change in PP&E	(10)
CFF	
Repurchases of Stock	(7)
Dividends	(2)
Total CFF	(9)
Total Change in Cash	3
Beginning Cash	10
Ending Cash	13

1C Calculate the below measures and ratios for the **Current Year only.**

	Previous Year	Current Year	
Gross Margin			(sales – cogs) / sales
EBIT			sales – cogs – sga – r&d – depreciation
EBIT Margin			ebit / sales
Profit Margin			net income / sales
Asset Turnover (using year end assets)			sales / total assets
Asset Turnover (using average assets)			sales / average total assets
Accounts Receivable Turnover			sales / ending accounts receivable
Days Sales Outstanding			365 / accounts receivable turnover
Inventory Turnover			cogs / ending inventory
Days Sales Inventory			365 / inventory turnover
Purchases			ending inventory + cogs – beginning inventory
Accounts Payable Turnover			purchases / ending accounts payable
Days Payable Outstanding			365 / accounts payable turnover
Assets to Equity			total assets / equity
Return on Equity (Net Income / Ending Equity)			net income / ending equity
Return on Equity (using the Dupont model)			profit margin * asset turnover * assets to equity
Current Ratio			current assets / current liabilities
Quick Ratio			(cash + accounts receivable) / current liabilities
Debt to Capital			interest bearing debt / (interest bearing debt + equity)
Interest Coverage			ebit / interest expense
Dividend Payout Ratio			dividends / net income
Effective Tax Rate			income tax expense / pre tax income
NOPAT			ebit * (1 – effective tax rate)
Year End Stock Price (given)	10	12	assumed
Number of Shares (given)		10	assumed
ROIC (based on market value of equity)			nopat / (interest bearing debt + market value of equity)
Effective Interest Rate (after tax)			interest expense * (1 – effective tax rate) / interest bearing debt
Market Capitalization			year end stock price * number of shares

| **1C** | Calculate the below measures and ratios for the **Current Year only**. |

	Previous Year	Current Year	
Gross Margin		0.400	(sales – cogs) / sales
EBIT		14.000	sales – cogs – sga – r&d – depreciation
EBIT Margin		0.070	ebit / sales
Profit Margin		0.030	net income / sales
Asset Turnover (using year end assets)		1.408	sales / total assets
Asset Turnover (using average assets)		1.370	sales / average total assets
Accounts Receivable Turnover		8.000	sales / ending accounts receivable
Days Sales Outstanding		45.625	365 / accounts receivable turnover
Inventory Turnover		12.000	cogs / ending inventory
Days Sales Inventory		30.417	365 / inventory turnover
Purchases		110.000	ending inventory + cogs – beginning inventory
Accounts Payable Turnover		7.333	purchases / ending accounts payable
Days Payable Outstanding		49.773	365 / accounts payable turnover
Assets to Equity		2.119	total assets / equity
Return on Equity (Net Income / Ending Equity)		0.090	net income / ending equity
Return on Equity (using the Dupont model)		0.090	profit margin * asset turnover * assets to equity
Current Ratio		3.200	current assets / current liabilities
Quick Ratio		2.533	(cash + accounts receivable) / current liabilities
Debt to Capital		0.472	interest bearing debt / (interest bearing debt + equity)
Interest Coverage		3.500	ebit / interest expense
Dividend Payout Ratio		0.333	dividends / net income
Effective Tax Rate		0.400	income tax expense / pre tax income
NOPAT		8.400	ebit * (1 – effective tax rate)
Year End Stock Price (given)	10	12	assumed
Number of Shares (given)		10	assumed
ROIC (based on market value of equity)		0.047	nopat / (interest bearing debt + market value of equity)
Effective Interest Rate (after tax)		0.040	interest expense * (1 – effective tax rate) / interest bearing debt
Market Capitalization		120.000	year end stock price * number of shares